ALA Editions · **SPECIAL REPORTS**

NARRATIVES OF (DIS)ENFRANCHISEMENT

Reckoning with the History of Libraries and the Black and African American Experience

TRACEY OVERBEY AND AMANDA L. FOLK

ALA
Editions
CHICAGO 2022

ALA Editions purchases fund advocacy, awareness, and accreditation programs for library professionals worldwide.

ISBNs
978-0-8389-3737-2 (paper)
978-0-8389-4992-4 (PDF)

Library of Congress Cataloging-in-Publication Data

Names: Overbey, Tracey, author. | Folk, Amanda L., author.
Title: Narratives of (dis)enfranchisement : reckoning with the history of libraries and the Black and African American experience / Tracey Overbey and Amanda L. Folk.
Description: Chicago : ALA Editions, 2022. | Series: ALA Editions special reports | Includes bibliographical references and index. | Summary: "This report provides an overview of the historical exclusion and disenfranchisement of Black Americans and African Americans from libraries and educational institutions in the United States and explores the ways in which the legacy of this exclusion manifests today" —Provided by publisher.
Identifiers: LCCN 2022018686 (print) | LCCN 2022018687 (ebook) | ISBN 9780838937372 (paperback) | ISBN 9780838949924 (pdf)
Subjects: LCSH: Libraries and Black people—United States. | African Americans and libraries. | Libraries—United States—History—20th century.
Classification: LCC Z711.9 .O94 2022 (print) | LCC Z711.9 (ebook) | DDC 027.0089/96073—dc23/eng/20220521
LC record available at https://lccn.loc.gov/2022018686
LC ebook record available at https://lccn.loc.gov/2022018687

Series cover design by Casey Bayer. Series text design in Palatino Linotype and Interstate by Karen Sheets de Gracia.

♾ This paper meets the requirements of ANSI/NISO Z39.48-1992 (Permanence of Paper).

Printed in the United States of America
26 25 24 23 22   5 4 3 2 1

CONTENTS

PREFACE

"Being American is more than a pride we inherit, it's the past we step into and how we repair it."—Amanda Gorman, *The Hill We Climb*

"I can't breathe."—Eric Garner

"Mama."—George Floyd

We believe it's important to place this book within our country's broader racial context, as it is this context that has inspired us to write this book and encourage our profession to consider what it means to confront racism in our libraries and communities and develop actionable antiracist agendas. We began this project in earnest in 2017. According to #Say Their Names (https://sayevery.name), eight Black and African American children and adults in six different states ranging in age from 15 to 66 were murdered by law enforcement or died in police custody that year. Damon Grimes. James Lacy. Charleena Lyles. Mikel McIntyre. Jordan Edwards. Timothy Caughman. Alteria Woods. Desmond Phillips. In 2018 that number almost doubled. Fourteen Black and African American children and adults in eight states ranging in age from 17 to 45 were murdered by law enforcement or died in police custody. Aleah Jenkins. Emantic Bradford Jr. Jemel Robinson. Charles Roundtree Jr. Botham Jean. Harith Augustus. Jason Washington. Antwon Rose Jr. Robert White. Earl McNeil. Marcus-David Peters. Danny Ray Thomas. Stephon Clark. Ronell Foster. In 2019 eleven Black and African American adults in seven different states ranging in age from 21 to 56 were murdered by law enforcement or died in police custody. John Neville. Michael Dean. Atatiana Jeff-

erson. Byron Williams. Elijah McClain. Jaleel Murdock. Dominique Clayton. Pamela Turner. Ronald Greene. Sterling Higgins. Bradley Blackshire. In 2019 a 66-year-old Atlanta librarian was pulled over in North Carolina for going 10 miles per hour over the speed limit. She did not realize that the police were attempting to pull her over, and they interpreted this as her attempting to run from them. When she realized what was happening and pulled over, officers pulled her out of her vehicle by her hair and threw her to the ground with their guns drawn on the side of the highway. All of this was caught on body camera video. At one point, one of the officers can be heard saying, "That's good police work, baby." So good that Ms. Bottom suffered a dislocated shoulder and torn rotator cuff that required surgery. At the time of writing, Ms. Bottom has filed a lawsuit against Salisbury (NC) City Police.

We decided to develop a book proposal to submit to ALA Editions in the summer of 2020. As we witnessed yet another unarmed Black man murdered by the police—George Floyd—and how the ensuing protests were met with militarized police forces across the country, we decided that writing this book was one small step that we could take in the fight for racial justice. Indeed, in Columbus, Ohio, we watched video footage of our own Black elected officials, including Congresswoman Joyce Beatty and City Council President Shannon Hardin, being pepper sprayed by the Columbus Division of Police as they exercised their First Amendment rights on public sidewalks downtown. Furthermore, we were in the midst of a global pandemic that was disproportionately affecting Black and African American communities. Due to a variety of factors, such as continued unequal access to health care, implicit bias in the provision of health care, and their overrepresentation in jobs considered to be essential, Black Americans and African Americans were 2.4 times more likely than White Americans to die as a result of COVID-19, according to an article published by the National Academies of Sciences, Engineering, and Medicine in July 2020 (Frueh, 2020).

As 2020 continued to unfold, the picture did not become more positive. Thirty-one Black and African American adults in 19 different states ranging in age from 18 to 60 were murdered by law enforcement or died in police custody. Bennie Edwards. Casey Goodson Jr. Kevin Peterson. Walter Wallace Jr. Jonathan Price. Kurt Reinhold. Dijon Kizzee. Damian Daniels. Anthony McClain. Julian Lewis. Maurice Abisdid-Wagner. Rayshard Brooks. Priscilla Slater. Kamal Flowers. Jamel Floyd. David McAtee. Calvin Horton Jr. Tony McDade. Dion Johnson. George Floyd. Maurice Gordon. Steven Taylor. Daniel Prude. Breonna Taylor. Barry Gedeus. Manuel Ellis. Lionel Morris. Jaquyn O'Neill Light. William Green. Darius Tarver. Miciah Lee. This list does not include Ahmaud Arbery, who was followed and murdered by White men in Georgia while he was out for a run. It took 74 days for an arrest to be made despite video evidence. This list also does not include Andre Hill, who was murdered by a Columbus (OH) police officer in his own driveway near the end of 2020. In between those two murders, a grand jury failed to indict the police officer who murdered Breonna Taylor as she slept in her own home.

We began a semester-long research leave to focus our energies on writing this book in January 2021, and 2021 seems to have been a continuation of 2020 in many ways. On the same day that Andre Hill was laid to rest—January 5, 2021—the Kenosha County (WI) District Attorney announced that they would not file charges against the officer who murdered Jacob Blake. The following day crowds of Trump supporters, who are predominantly White, began to gather at the Capitol in Washington, DC, to protest the certification of the presidential election results. Even though there was advance warning of protests, the footage showed very little law enforcement present, a remarkable contrast to protests across the country in support of Black lives and racial justice, which were often met with scores of police in riot gear and occasionally the National Guard. A failed insurrection at the Capitol ensued. On April 20, 2021, the officer who murdered George Floyd was found guilty on three counts—second-degree unintentional murder, second-degree manslaughter, and third-degree manslaughter. Even though this verdict could not bring George Floyd back to life, many celebrated the fact that a police officer was finally being held to account for murdering a Black man. This celebration was short-lived, as a Columbus (OH) police officer killed 16-year-old Ma'Khia Bryant while she was in an altercation that included a knife. Just hours following her death, there was video footage of other Columbus (OH) police officers telling neighborhood residents that blue lives matter. While there has been controversy about whether or not her death was warranted (it was not), because she had a knife, it stands in stark contrast to a long list of White men who have committed mass murders and were peacefully taken into custody even while heavily armed. The day after that, Andre Brown Jr. was killed by police officers in Elizabeth City, North Carolina, while sitting in his vehicle in his driveway with his hands on the steering wheel. At the time of writing, 10 additional Black and African American adults in eight different states ranging in age from 18 to 52 have already been murdered by law enforcement or died in police custody. Matthew "Zadok" Williams. Daunte Wright. James Lionel Johnson. Dominique Williams. Marvin Scott III. Jenoah Donald. Patrick Warren. Xzavier Hill. Robert Howard. Vincent Belmonte.

Through our complementary special reports, the one that follows and *Narratives of (Dis)Engagement: Exploring Black and African American Students' Experiences in Libraries*, we hope to demonstrate the ways in which both systemic racism and implicit bias affect our profession. Many like to tout libraries as neutral spaces because we uphold the ideals of democracy and provide free access to all. However, libraries are not neutral spaces, and the reproduction of that narrative results in unequal service to different user populations. As is explained in more depth in this special report, libraries and the institutions with which they are associated have a long history of racial exclusion. Furthermore, as we discuss in *Narratives of (Dis) Engagement*, few studies have explored the ways in which the legacy of that exclusion manifests in contemporary libraries for those who are Black, Indigenous, and People of Color (BIPOC). These complementary special reports are an initial attempt at filling that gap, beginning a conversation, and creating a call to action.

One of the authors, Tracey, once heard a trainer offering an equity, diversity, and inclusion workshop say something like, "Who owns the earth? We all have to breathe." As a profession, we need to make sure that we are providing environments that offer for all of our diverse user populations and professional colleagues the space to breathe and to thrive.

ACKNOWLEDGMENTS

Many people directly or indirectly made this report a reality, and we would like to take some space to say thank you to them.

FROM BOTH TRACEY AND AMANDA

We thank Damon Jaggars, Vice Provost and Dean of The Ohio State University Libraries, for providing us with funding to conduct this research study, as well as a special assignment for both of us to concentrate our energies on writing this special report. We thank Damon also for his unwavering support for this project in general and for providing us with a safe environment in which to do this work. We also thank our supervisors, Deidra Herring and Alison Armstrong, for their unconditional support of research and writing related to this project, including allowing us to apply for and take a special assignment in 2021. We thank our University Libraries colleagues more generally for encouraging our research and scholarship related to this topic.

We thank several colleagues for providing us with thoughtful and useful feedback on early drafts of chapters—Dr. Renee Hill, Dr. Sandra Hughes-Hassell, Dr. Kafi Kumasi, Nichole Shabazz, and Shaunda Vasudev. We appreciate the time, labor, and expertise that you were willing to share with us. We also thank the Tulsa City-County Library Research Center, particularly Nick Abrahamson, for their willingness to provide us with documentation related to the Tulsa Race Massacre and the Archer Street Library.

Finally, we thank our acquisitions editor at ALA Editions, Rachel Chance, for enthusiastically believing in our project and providing us with guidance and feedback throughout this process. If it were not for Rachel, this special report would not be a reality. We are grateful for your support!

FROM TRACEY

Participating in this type of study has shed so much light, providing insight into and awareness of the many contributions and struggles of people of Black and African American ancestry and their contributions to society and the world that have gone hidden, unnoticed, and unacknowledged. I would like to honor known and unknown Black and African American ancestors who created civilizations and institutions, who went unacknowledged for their contributions to the world. I would like to say thank you for setting a blueprint for many civilizations to follow.

I thank my colleague, research partner, and coauthor, Dr. Amanda Folk, for being brave, inquisitive, and bold enough to peer inside a little bit of what has been hidden within Black and African American ancestry history. You have viewed and examined the research, more than most have done, and have been humble enough to acknowledge it within our publication. I am very grateful for you reaching out to me, in a setting that had only a few who looked like me, to ask if we could work together on a very sensitive topic like race and libraries. My hope is that the information which we have shared will be continued in academic librarianship by new and upcoming librarians—who will be just as brave and honest as you have been to uncover those hidden truths about the Black and African American experiences with libraries.

I thank my mother, Annie Mcgrady, for her absolute devotion in guiding me toward education and seeking knowledge. You explained to me very early how the world sees our people and how I must change that narrative through education. You have been a great example for me to follow. I appreciate all the many settings you placed me in that had many races and ethnicities. I truly appreciate the sacrifices and love you have shown me throughout my life. I also thank my dad, Wash Allen; I thank you for being my secret motivator! You have always lit the fire in me to keep me going when I wanted to give up. I am ever grateful for being your daughter and for the love you have shown me through my life.

I thank my husband, my best friend and confidant, Edward E. Overbey Jr. You have always supported me—on every venture I conjure. I appreciate all the encouragement, spiritual insights, and love. You champion me when no one sees the struggle; you are a fantastic partner and an excellent father and human being; a woman could not ask for more in a mate. I would also like to acknowledge my children, Rodney Maurice Williams Jr and Asa Khalil Overbey. Rodney, although you transitioned at a young age, I know you are my angel, watching over me and helping me along my life purpose. I miss you so much; not a day goes by that I do not think about you and feel your spirit. Asa, I'm so grateful you chose me to be your mother; it has been an honor to raise you and watch you grow into this bright, funny, loving engineer that you want to become. Please know this is all for you, and my grandchildren one day.

I would also like to shout out family members who have passed on, but who are never forgotten and whose shoulders I stand on today. My grandparents Chester and Annie Ruth Mcgrady, who taught me consistency and perseverance. To my late uncle bug, Chester Mcgrady Jr, Cynthia Horton (auntie), Lawrence and Brian Adam Mcgrady (cousins), and last but not least my great-great grandmother (big ma) Sallie Mcgrady. To my living family and friends who have stood by me in test of times during this journey. My brother, Michael McCall, I appreciate you always

reaching out and encouraging me and my family to strive higher and be the best we can be. My dear sister, Wykema Morse, I have watched you over time, you inspire me so much; I love you so dearly. To my dear friend since elementary school Monica Daniely, we have cried and achieved together, I appreciate the honest and empowering talks. Last but not least, my dearest friend Kimberly Granger-Cummings (my ride or die), although we don't talk often, I truly appreciate the support you have given me throughout this journey called life. I truly miss you.

I also thank mentors in my life who have encouraged me on this journey in academia. Dr. Rena Mae Baker, you have been a great mentor, and role model, who encourages me often that I can do this, and that my experiences are needed within the scholarship arena for academic libraries. Deidra Herring, I truly appreciate your leadership in sparking the fire in me through academic libraries.

FROM AMANDA

I first thank my research partner and coauthor, Tracey Overbey. I don't know what it was that made you trust me when I suggested this research project, but I will be eternally grateful to you for taking this risk. Our research has been one of the high points of my career, and I believe our shared accomplishments will be those of which I am most proud. This work has been some of the most meaningful and rewarding work of my career. It was not your responsibility to educate me, but I have learned so much from you that has made me a better librarian and person. I thank you so much for your willingness to work together, and I'm really looking forward to shaping our next project together!

I thank my parents, Dan and Cindy Folk, for your unconditional love and support in everything that I do, personally and professionally. While I have a lot of growth to do as an antiracist and White ally, you taught me from an early age that it is important to have friends who are different from you. As I reflect on my own experiences, being in a diverse day care setting was foundational, as some of the earliest friends that I can remember making were African

American or biracial. I didn't realize how unusual that was until I was much older.

I thank my husband and best friend, Allen Perry. You believe in me more than I believe in myself, and you support me even when I take on projects that require so much of me that there is little left of me to devote to other things. Thank you for always being there for me, telling me that I am capable of accomplishing my goals, keeping my feet on the ground, reminding me to take a moment to breathe, and for learning alongside me.

I thank Dr. Linda DeAngelo, not only for being an amazing mentor, but also for modeling what it means to be an antiracist scholar and White ally. You have given me the tools to embark on this journey, and I wouldn't be the scholar that I am today without you. I am so grateful for you and your continued support.

I'm also fortunate to have so many close friends and colleagues who have helped me along this journey as mentors and peers in the learning process. Thank you so much to Maria Accardi, Dr. Sheila Confer, Sandra Enimil, Pamela Espinosa de los Monteros, Jenn Grimmett, Pema Lin, Marley Nelson, Z Tenney, Dr. Erika Pryor, Jessica Riviere, and (last, but definitely not least!) Dr. Gretchen Underwood-Schaefer. I also thank my running besties who shared many miles with me throughout this process—Tom Anderson, Jess Moomaw, Morgan Myers, Becca Rohner, and Renata Weaver.

1

INTRODUCTION

In this report, we provide an overview of the historical exclusion and disenfranchisement of Black Americans and African Americans from libraries and educational institutions in the United States and explore the ways in which the legacy of this exclusion is manifest in our contemporary context. This overview is not meant to be comprehensive, definitive, or authoritative. Rather, we hope that this overview serves as the beginning of many conversations in which our profession reckons with our racist past to create a more equitable, antiracist future. In our complementary report, *Narratives of (Dis)Engagement: Exploring Black and African American Students' Experiences in Libraries,* we introduce the findings of a research study that highlights the public, school, and academic library experiences of Black and African American college students. We examine the role that race has played in their library experiences to identify potential opportunities for libraries to better meet the needs of these users whose voices and experiences are not often represented in our professional literature. Although we hope both special reports are read together, we have written each report such that they can also stand alone.

THE OVERWHELMING WHITENESS OF LIBRARIANSHIP IN THE UNITED STATES

This section's heading is a play on a well-known blog post from Chris Bourg, Director of Libraries at the Massachusetts Institute of Technology (MIT), titled "The Unbearable Whiteness of Librarianship" (Bourg, 2014). In this post, Bourg compares the demographics of the profession to that of the US population using the 2010 ALA Diversity Counts data and 2013 US census data. Not surprisingly, she found significant differences in terms of racial representation. According to the census data, about 63 percent of the population was White in 2013. However, the ALA data indicated that 88 percent of librarians at that time were White. Furthermore, Black Americans and African Americans comprised 15 percent of the population but only 5 percent of librarians. At that time, Bourg writes that the profession would need more than 11,000 Black or African American librarians to bring the profession to representational parity with the population of the United States. In 2018–19, just under 6,700 master's degrees in library and information science (LIS) were awarded (ALISE, 2020). Even if every new LIS graduate were Black or African American, it would still take two years for the profession to reach representational parity with the overall population.

Unfortunately, there has not been much progress in recruiting and retaining Black and African American librarians (or BIPOC librarians more generally) in the past decade. The American Library Association (ALA) conducted a membership survey in 2017, and about 75 percent of members responded. In both 2014 and 2017, the percentage of White librarians remained steady at about 87 percent, and Black and African American librarians comprised just over 4 percent of the membership in those years (Rosa & Henke, 2017). More recent data from the Department for Professional Employees (2020) of the AFL-CIO (American Federation of Labor and Congress of Industrial Organizations) shows a slight decrease in the number of White librarians (83 percent), but the percentage of Black and African American librarians remained relatively static at 5 percent. Indeed, the most recent Statistical Report from the Association of Library and Information Science Education (ALISE, 2020) indicates that current enrollment in ALA-accredited master of library science programs will continue to reproduce these same demographics. In 2019 the enrollment percentage of Black and African American students mirrored that of the profession at approximately 5 percent. However, White students comprised just 62 percent of students enrolled in these programs. Their overall representation in master's programs being lower than in the workforce is likely due to the presence of international students (4 percent) and students whose race or ethnicity is unknown (13 percent), rather than a dramatic shift in overall demographics of emerging professionals.

You might be questioning why these demographics matter if we, as library professionals and paraprofessionals, have made the commitment to serve all the members of our communities regardless of race or ethnicity. Although this commitment might be genuine, many White librarians are likely unaware of their own implicit and learned biases, the ways in which race affects the daily lives of BIPOC, and may not feel the need to acknowledge or address the legacies of our profession's historical racial exclusion and disenfranchisement of Black and African American communities. Many White people in the United States currently take a color-blind or color-evasive approach to

race, meaning that they think it is better (or more polite or comfortable) to avoid acknowledging race. This approach might be deployed with good intentions, but it ends up maintaining White supremacy and toxicity in the long term. We discuss this more in the sections that follow.

CONFRONTING WHITENESS IN LIBRARIES

We have written this book with all librarians and library staff in mind. However, we believe that there will be different key takeaways for the reader based on their race or ethnicity. In this book, we are attempting to balance a desire to educate and inform a predominantly White profession about the racialized realities that many of our BIPOC colleagues and users have faced and still face in libraries, as well as in the educational institutions with which they are associated, with our desire to empower, reaffirm, and validate the experiences of our BIPOC colleagues and users. The former goal, to educate and inform, may result in a rehashing of what is likely a tired refrain that our BIPOC colleagues know all too well—that BIPOC students, particularly Black and African American students, face a variety of challenges throughout their educational experiences that result in persistent equity gaps. However, many White readers might be unaware of and shocked by the extent to which the legacy of our country's racialized past is present today and the ways in which this past continues to disenfranchise and oppress BIPOC. Our goal is not to approach BIPOC communities from a deficit frame. Rather, we intend to uncover how this is a failure of the institutions, which were built on the foundation of White supremacy over several centuries, and not a failure of BIPOC students, their families, and their communities. In the chapters that follow, we intend to demonstrate how our institutions were never built as environments in which BIPOC students were meant to thrive, and the legacy of these foundations built on intentional and systemic racism is still present today and urgently needs to be addressed by everyone, but especially by White people who hold significant power and privilege. Although we have written this book with all librarians and library staff in mind, we hope that our White readers will find this to be a compelling call to action to identify and dismantle manifestations of White supremacy in their libraries and in their individual practice.

Tracie D. Hall, who is the current executive director of ALA, once wrote, "the library and information science field has seemingly slapped itself with a gag order [about race and racism]. While the discussion of diversity in libraries has proliferated over the past few decades, meaningful dialogue around race has been eviscerated or altogether evaded" (Hall, 2012, p. 198). With these words in mind, we contend that our profession has not directly confronted the racialized histories of libraries, including the educational institutions with which they are associated, to explore and uncover how race continues to shape the experiences of our contemporary library users. This evasion is likely a result of the overwhelming Whiteness of the profession. Race remains largely invisible to most White people because they do not go through the same process of racial identity formation that BIPOC do due to the cultural normalization of Whiteness (Tatum, 2017). Because of this, issues related to race and the manifestation of Whiteness and White supremacy in all facets of the lives of BIPOC, including their work (library) lives, remain invisible to most White people. In addition, the United States remains highly racially segregated, even today. Most White people do not have meaningful interactions with BIPOC on a regular basis, which has an impact on their ability to relate to BIPOC (Feagin, 2020). This creates uncomfortable interactions, and the discomfort is only heightened when the topic of the interactions includes race. As White people become more aware of the presence of White supremacy and toxicity and their complicity in it, common reactions include shutting down and avoiding the topic to maintain comfort; dismissing it as irrelevant or learned victimization; reverting to phrases like "I don't see color," "I'm not a racist," or "You misunderstood. I'm a good person"; or becoming paralyzed by guilt (Tatum, 2017). None of these reactions are productive in terms of dismantling White supremacy and toxicity and moving toward a more equitable and just world.

Although there has been some research exploring the experiences of Black and African American library

users, which we discuss in the coming chapters, there is a lack of research that explores how race affects their experiences in libraries. This is critical given the overwhelming Whiteness of librarianship previously discussed. BIPOC experience racism and discrimination on a regular and frequent basis as they attempt to live their lives. We have no reason to believe that when BIPOC users pass through the doors of our buildings or enter our virtual spaces that they suddenly enter a race-neutral zone. Furthermore, BIPOC users do not shed their racialized identities when they are in our spaces; they bring their whole selves to the library, including the racism and discrimination that they experience with regularity in nonlibrary spaces. We cannot expect that they perceive a White person at the reference or circulation desk differently because they are in a library space. Because we do not have a basic understanding of how race affects library users' experiences, our profession is maintaining White supremacy while also espousing values related to diversity, inclusivity, equity, and social justice. The late Maya Angelou once said, "Do the best you can until you know better. Then when you know better, do better." We hope that this special report provides an opportunity for our profession to know better and do better by our BIPOC users, colleagues, and communities.

RACE AND RACISM IN THE UNITED STATES

For centuries, racial categories were treated as if they were a biological or scientific reality. On the one hand, this likely makes sense to many people, as we are able to see clear physical differences among people of different races, such as skin color or hair texture. However, race is a social construct and is not a biological reality. Indeed, "genetic variation within so-called racial groups is much greater than the variation between them" (Goodman, 2008, p. 6). Instead, racial categories were created by Europeans during the age of exploration and colonization to justify, both morally and scientifically, the subjugation of those whom they were colonizing (Feagin, 2020; Kendi, 2019). These categorizations eventually evolved into a "great chain of being," or a racial hierarchy that put White men at the top and BIPOC at the bottom (Feagin, 2020).

Feagin (2020) writes, "In this framework a natural order is mapped onto a moral order. Persisting social inequalities are viewed as natural and legitimate" (p. 53). It was this hierarchical racial categorization that enabled chattel slavery and land theft, as well as Jim Crow laws and customs. It bears repeating, however, that this kind of categorization has no scientific backing. It is not a biological reality.

Before discussing how racism manifests in the United States today and what that means for our profession, it is necessary for us to articulate how we define racism. Oluo (2019) provides an excellent starting point: "A prejudice against someone based on race, when those prejudices are reinforced by systems of power" (p. 27). There are two important elements to this definition—an individual element and a systemic element—both of which are harmful and insidious. All people, regardless of their race, hold prejudices and biases, which can manifest regularly, intentionally or not. These can be overt, such as using a racial slur or committing an act of violence. They can also be subtle, such as giving a backhanded compliment (e.g., telling a Black person how articulate they are as if you did not expect that) or asking an ignorant question (e.g., asking an Asian American person what country they are from). Sometimes the offender is completely unaware that they are being offensive, though the result for the receiver is the same regardless of intent. However, it is the "reinforced by systems of power" element that really gives racism its teeth. This means that racial oppression is built into key institutions of our country, including education, government, law enforcement and criminal justice, banking, and health care. This kind of racism advantages White people, especially White people of particular social classes, and disadvantages BIPOC. Systemic racism is why our neighborhoods and cities continue to remain racially segregated; why Black women are more likely to die during childbirth; why White children are more likely to attend and graduate from college; why Black men are more likely to receive harsher sentences than White men for the same crime; why White people are more likely to accumulate generational wealth; and why police officers can murder

unarmed Black people and not be held accountable. Identifying and acknowledging the systemic nature of racism that upholds White privilege and power is critical in determining an antiracist agenda. There are many White people who do not hold explicit racist views, do not use racial slurs, and believe in the values of diversity and inclusivity. However, if those same White people do not actively fight to dismantle oppressive systems of racial power, then they are complicit in upholding White supremacy and toxicity. This is how it is possible to have racism without racists (Bonilla-Silva, 2018; Oluo, 2019).

Scholarship about race in the United States from various disciplines, including sociology, political science, education, and economics, has identified a shift in how racism manifests in our society since the Civil Rights era. As many readers likely know, prior to the Civil Rights era in the 1960s, racism against Black and African American citizens was overt, direct, and typically violent, including enslavement, segregation, and lynching. However, many scholars believe that we have shifted to a new racism since the 1960s, a more subtle and coded form of racism that is predicated on a color-blind ideology. While the predominant phrase used in the scholarship on this topic is *color-blind ideology*, we use the phrase *color-evasive ideology* for two reasons. First, the term *color-blind ideology* is ableist and "equates blindness with ignorance" (Annamma et al., 2017, p. 154). Second, "colorblindness implies passivity," which "allows for a justification of inaction that propels the system of racial inequities forward" (p. 154). A color-evasive ideology is one that espouses the belief that race is no longer relevant to understanding society or that it is somehow racist to be aware of and acknowledge race. This latter point may even seem virtuous, in that one may believe that choosing not to acknowledge race somehow results in equality. However, the reason why color-evasive ideologies are harmful is that they often serve as "an assertion of equal opportunity that minimizes the reality of racism in favor of individual or cultural explanations of reality" (Burke, 2019, p. 2). In other words, it denies both the racialized experiences that BIPOC have with prejudiced individuals as well as the very existence of systemic racism, shifting the blame to BIPOC for perceived (and inaccurate) cultural deficits.

Public opinion research has demonstrated gaps in how White Americans and Black Americans/African Americans perceive the prevalence of racism in the United States. A Pew Research Center survey found a 15 percent difference between White and Black participants in response to the statement "race relations in the U.S. are generally bad," with 56 percent of White people agreeing and 71 percent of Black people agreeing (Horowitz et al., 2019). However, 50 percent of White respondents indicated that they believed too much attention is given to race, a belief that only 12 percent of Black respondents shared. Furthermore, 52 percent of White respondents believed that people see racial discrimination where it does not exist. Despite this, 54 percent of White respondents believed that racial discrimination was a major reason why Black people have a hard time getting ahead, although a more common reason was less access to good schools (60 percent). Fifty-nine percent of White respondents believed that focusing on what all races have in common improved race relations compared to just 44 percent of Black respondents. These troubling statistics provide some evidence for the prevalence of a color-evasive ideology.

The LIS profession has been critiqued for its race-evasive approach to diversity, equity, and inclusivity, as alluded to in the earlier quote from Hall (2012). Pawley (2006) concurs, arguing that "substituting multiculturalism and diversity for race allows the library community to evade confronting racism as—still—a defining dimension of American society and, in this way, helps perpetuate it" (p. 153). Over a decade later, Hudson (2017) penned a critique on the continued focus on diversity, particularly representational diversity, at the expense of "meaningful inclusion" (p. 10). Rather than interrogating the ways in which systemic racism and White supremacy continue to manifest in libraries, our profession has focused primarily on cultural competence training, which encourages individuals to work together respectfully and harmoniously. The development of

cultural competence, although important, is not enough to combat racism in our profession. Furthermore, there have been critiques that the LIS profession has participated in performative antiracist politics in response to the continued and frequent incidents of police brutality and murder of Black Americans and African Americans in the United States. Mehra (2021) discusses how these antiracist performances appear to be inauthentic and insincere because the profession has largely ignored is own racist history, preferring a sanitized version of library history that does not include the perpetuation of White supremacy.

STRUCTURE OF THIS REPORT

In the chapters that follow, we intend to provide an overview of libraries' historical complicity with racial exclusion and disenfranchisement of Black Americans and African Americans in the United States and discuss the contemporary legacies of these exclusionary practices. Furthermore, we discuss contemporary scholarship related to Black and African American users' experiences with libraries. We intend for the following chapters to provide a historical and contemporary contextualization of the research findings that we present in *Narratives of (Dis) Engagement*. In addition, we do not intend for these overviews to be comprehensive or definitive, as this is outside the scope of these special reports. We hope that this report will help the LIS profession reckon with its racist past and the implications for how we meet the needs of diverse user communities today and in the future. In other words, we intend for this report to be a conversation starter, in terms of both our professional practice (e.g., building collections, developing programming, and helping patrons with their information needs) and also our scholarship, assessment, and evaluation practices.

We begin this overview with a chapter that describes the hidden history of Africa's contributions to libraries and educational institutions. These contributions, more often than not, are omitted from our K–12, higher education, and library school curricula. We then proceed with overviews of three different library types—public, school (K–12), and academic libraries. These chapters are followed by a discussion about frameworks and theories that can help us to identify and unpack the role of race in our profession and our users' experiences. The concluding chapter discusses some practical takeaways based on the preceding chapters.

RECOMMENDED READING

Curry, D. A. (1994). Your worries ain't like mine: African American librarians and the pervasiveness of racism, prejudice and discrimination in academe. *The Reference Librarian*, 21(45–46), 299–311.

Horowitz, J. M., Brown, A., & Cox, K. (2019, April 9). *Race in America 2019*. Pew Research Center. https://www.pewresearch.org/social-trends/2019/04/09/race-in-america-2019/

Jackson, A. P., Jefferson, J. C., & Nosakhere, A. S. (Eds.) (2012). *The 21st-century Black librarian in America: Issues and challenges*. Scarecrow Press.

Mehra, B. (2021). Enough crocodile tears! Libraries moving beyond performative antiracist politics. *Library Quarterly*, 91(2), 137–149.

2

THE AFRICAN ROOTS OF EDUCATION AND LIBRARIANSHIP

W hen one conjures an image of the earliest institutions of learning, including libraries, one might picture medieval European universities—Bologna, Oxford, Sala-
manca, Cambridge, Padua. One might also think about the great minds that predated
the creation of the formal universities—inventors, astronomers, orators, artists. For
many of us, these great minds are likely White, European men. Rarely do we learn
about African contributions to the origins of education, scientific and artistic knowledge, and librarianship. There is a long history of ignoring the contributions of Africans
and African Americans to the development of educational institutions and knowledge
creation more generally. Most of us likely did not learn about the rich African contributions to the foundations of knowledge, unless we took courses on African history in
college. Relying heavily on Zulu (1993), we provide an overview of these contributions
and explore the African roots of education and librarianship.

The oldest, continuously operated university in the world is located in Africa—the
University of Al-Karaouine (also Al-Quaraouiyine or Al-Qarawiyyin) in Fez, Morocco
(Griffiths & Buttery, 2018). Founded in 859 AD, the University of Al-Karaouine was a
religious center for Muslims as well as a place of learning that included the study of
"linguistics, grammar, law, music, Sufism, medicine and astronomy" (Griffiths & Buttery, 2018). The library was expanded in the 1300s and has become significant in the
Muslim world due to its collections, which include "some of the oldest preserved man-
uscripts in Islamic history" (Griffiths & Buttery, 2018). Timbuktu, in present-day Mali,
was also known as a center for learning under the reign of Mansa Musa I during the
twelfth century. Similar to Al-Karaouine, the University of Timbuktu (or the University
of Sankore) was a site of religious study and higher learning (MacDonald, n.d.). In
addition to Islamic theology, scholars in Timbuktu studied "law, grammar, rhetoric,
logic, history, geography, astronomy, . . . astrology," and medicine (Cartwright, 2019).

Many readers are likely more familiar with ancient Egypt and its contributions to
intellectual traditions. However, many people associate Egypt with the Middle East
rather than Africa, even though Egypt is clearly part of the African continent. The
ancient Egyptians referred to their country as Kemet[1] or "the black land" (Zulu, 1993, p.
246). While some have attributed this name to the color of the soil in the region, Zulu
(1993) provides ample evidence that this name could be associated with the people
who lived there, including depictions of the ancient Kemetians and references to their
appearance in various documents, such as the Bible and the writings of Herodotus and

Aristotle. Therefore, it is important to explicitly acknowledge that the history of ancient Egypt is also part of the history of ancient Africa. Zulu (1993) writes,

> The crux of the issue of race and the Egyptians is part of an attempt to take Egypt and the Egyptian history out of Africa intellectually, and thus substitute a Euro-centric politicization of history that confirms the racist notion that Africa has no history of importance, and that the ancient civilization of Egypt is not part of the African experience, but rather is a part of the Arab, Asian, or Eurocentric experience. (p. 247)

As we discuss in the following chapters, many school curricula covering Black and African American history typically teach enslavement, segregation, and the Civil Rights movement and do not cover the important contributions that Africans have made to civilization over many centuries. Although we focus more on education in this chapter, African civilizations, such as Nubia, played important roles in economic development as well. This anemic approach to Black and African American history likely has a negative effect on the self-esteem of Black and African American children and denies all children the opportunity to receive a complete and accurate historical education. Indeed, King (2016) states,

> It is a formative, emotional, psychological mistake to introduce the history of black people with them as subjugated, enslaved peoples. Yes, it's simply inaccurate, it does damage—not just to young black children, but to all children, when they are given the distinct impression that black people began as inferior subjects and somehow found their way out.

Ancient Kemet was famous for its Mystery School, which was "designed to ensure (1) an educated leadership and (2) peace among the populous via effective leadership" (Zulu, 1993, p. 254). The Mystery School offered a robust curriculum, including the study of "medicine, science, astronomy, mathematics," "grammar, rhetoric, logic, geometry, arithmetic, [and] harmony/music" (p. 254). Because of this, people from around the ancient world traveled to study at the Mystery School, particularly ancient Greeks. The goal of the Mystery School—to develop leaders that would allow societies to thrive—is aligned with African indigenous knowledge. African indigenous knowledge has a "strong orientation to collective values and harmony rooted in a collective sense of responsibility—a 'collective ethic'—which acknowledges that survival of the group derives from harmony through interdependence and interconnectedness" (Owusu-Ansah & Mji, 2013, p. 2).

Because the language of ancient Egypt—hieroglyphics—is one of the oldest written languages,[2] the ancient Egyptians were early pioneers in written literature, including writings on both papyrus and stone tablets (Zulu, 1993). These early intellectual contributions created a need for libraries to collect, house, and organize literature, meaning that "Egyptian librarianship has a 6,000 year continuous history" (Zulu, 1993, p. 250). Like other ancient African and European universities and libraries, these early libraries often had a religious affiliation and were located in temples. Indeed, several scholars believe that the first library was located in ancient Kemet, perhaps established by Ramses II. Ramses II built several libraries in ancient Kemet, including "the Hypostyle Hall at Karnak, the Abu Simbel rock temple-library (regarded as one of the wonders of the world), the Abydos temple library, [and] the temple-library at Luxor" (Zulu, 1993, p. 251). He believed the library to be the "Medicine for the Soul," a motto that he had inscribed at the Ramesseum funerary temple-library at Thebes. Zulu describes how classification systems based on the Mystery System were used to catalog, organize, and retrieve materials in the libraries.

Another ancient Egyptian library has garnered more recognition than these earlier temple-libraries—the Great Library of Alexandria, which was part of the Musaeum (also spelled Mouseion). The Musaeum is one of the earliest research institutions, and, as such, it required an extensive library. The goal was to collect "all the books in the world," though the majority of the collection was likely ancient Greek writings followed by works of Egyptian priests (El-Abbadi, n.d.). The cataloging of materials was different from that of the Mystery System, which categorized materials based on "class (fire, water, earth, air), process (hot, cold, wet, dry), method (duality/union of opposites), and logic" (Zulu, 1993, p. 258). Instead, the Library of Alexandria developed the *Pinakes* to organize the collection, which included the following classifications: "rhetoric, law, epic, tragedy, comedy, lyric poetry, history, medicine, mathematics, natural science, and miscellaneous." In addition, to form the catalog, scribes recorded the following for the works contained in the library: the "work's title, author, and editor as well as its place of origin, length

(in lines), and whether the manuscript was mixed (containing more than one work) or unmixed (a single text)" (El-Abbadi, n.d.).

NOTES

1. We use ancient Kemet and ancient Egypt interchangeably in this chapter.
2. According to the British Library, both hieroglyphics and cuneiform, a written language developed in ancient Mesopotamia, were invented at roughly the same time (Clayton, n.d.).

3
PUBLIC LIBRARIES

OVERVIEW

In this chapter, we discuss the history of public libraries in the United States, paying particular attention to the exclusion of Black and African American communities through the mid-twentieth century. This history provides important context for thinking about the ways in which public libraries service Black and African American users and communities today. We then review literature, although scant, about Black and African American users' experiences with contemporary public libraries. This chapter provides a contextual foundation for the public library experiences of the students who participated in our research study, which we share in *Narratives of (Dis)Engagement: Exploring Black and African American Students' Experiences in Libraries*, including the importance of family in their library experiences and their identities as voracious readers.

THE HISTORICAL CONTEXT

Many consider public libraries to be a cornerstone of a functioning democracy, as they provide access to information regardless of an individual's ability to pay. These core principles are outlined in ALA's *Library Bill of Rights*, which was originally written in 1939 and has been amended six times through 2019. The *Library Bill of Rights* highlights access to information that represents multiple perspectives and the importance of privacy and intellectual freedom. Though the *Library Bill of Rights* extends to all libraries in the United States, the defining characteristics of public libraries are particularly apparent. The bill states that libraries are meant to serve the public, including individuals with diverse personal characteristics, such as their "origin, age, background, or views." However, this statement was not added until 1961. Prior to 1961, and in some cases after, White librarians, with the implicit support of ALA, denied many people of color the rights outlined in this document. The title of Knott's (2015) book about public libraries in the Jim Crow South reminds us that public libraries have a history of being "not free, not for all." Public libraries' tense and antagonistic history with communities of color, particularly the Black and African American community, has been well documented.

Until relatively recently, the intersections of race, racism, and libraries have largely been ignored in LIS, including the ways in which these intersections affect the profession today. Honma (2005) discusses the racialized history of public libraries in the United States to "[interrogate] the epistemological foundations of library science and [challenge] normativity, or more specifically the white racial normativity" in LIS (The

Omission of Color section, para. 2). To facilitate his interrogation, Honma examines the history of public libraries in the United States and the ways in which their historical development was racialized. Using the Boston Public Library, one of the first public libraries in the United States, as an example, Honma argues that a primary purpose of the public library was to assimilate new immigrants to White culture: "Thus, from its very inception, the public library system was engaged in a racializing project, one whose purpose was to inculcate European ethnics [i.e., Eastern and Southern European immigrants] into whiteness" (Honma, 2005, Library Ontologies and the Construction of Whiteness section, para. 5). This racializing project was done under the guise of democracy, which may seem like a noble cause. However, it set parameters for what was considered to be appropriate and acceptable for citizens of the United States, causing marginalized people, particularly people of color, to assimilate or acculturate to Whiteness. In other words, librarians have been "agents of authority and social control" in the "racial and racist" history of public libraries (Honma, 2005, Library Ontologies and the Construction of Whiteness section, para. 2). Honma argues for the importance of recognizing and acknowledging the transgressions of the past to move to a more equitable future.

Knott (2015) describes what this public-library-as-racializing-project phenomenon meant for African Americans in the first half of the twentieth century. Though she focuses her research primarily on the South, she includes accounts from other geographic regions as well. Private social and literary clubs played a significant role in the establishment of public libraries. Though these clubs did exist for Black Americans and African Americans, the powerful and influential clubs were primarily for White people only. In the early twentieth century, Andrew Carnegie began funding the development of public libraries that would be free and open to the public. Although he ultimately did support the provision of library services to Black and African American communities, he did not fight against segregated library services that were common in the South. Knott notes that different cities and regions each handled the establishment of

public libraries in different ways, but typically their establishment resulted in either the rejection or restriction of Black Americans and African Americans, including charging membership fees or not allowing Black Americans and African Americans to access public libraries by law.

Frequently branch libraries dedicated to Black Americans and African Americans were established, though funding for such a branch might have been the responsibility of the Black and African American community, even if the city or region had received external funding (e.g., money from philanthropists like Carnegie or Pratt) for the establishment of the main (White) public library. In some cases, the Black and African American community raised funds to establish their own independent library with no affiliation to the local public library system. Some of the Black and African American literary groups that existed in the late nineteenth and early twentieth centuries turned into Black independent libraries (Beasley, 2017) that served the community when public libraries would not. Similar to the issue of funding and resourcing of public schools based on which children they served, these segregated branches were separate and unequal (see box 3.1). The publicly funded branches available to Black and African American communities were often much smaller in size—both in terms of physical space and collections—and frequently contained discarded materials from the White branches. In addition, there were debates about who should run these branches—Black and African American librarians and staff or White librarians and staff. In some cases, White librarians promoted the erroneous belief that Black Americans and African Americans were less capable of fulfilling the roles and duties of librarians.

Though the acceptance, restriction, or outright exclusion of Black Americans and African Americans by public libraries tended to be a local or regional decision, the profession, including ALA, was complicit in enabling these practices and upholding White supremacy (Wiegand, 2017; Wiegand & Wiegand, 2018). In 1921, the ALA Work with Negroes Round Table was established to "examine the state of equitable access to library materials for African-Americans" (http://www.ala.org/aboutala/1920s). However, this initiative was short-lived and disbanded after just two years due to differing opinions about segregation and libraries. In 1925, ALA, in collaboration with the Carnegie Corporation, agreed to support the education of Black librarians at Virginia's Hampton Institute, so they could serve the "colored branches of city library systems" (Wiegand, 2017, p. 2). The National Association for the Advancement of Colored People (NAACP) disagreed with and protested this action, indicating that it would further segregate the profession and libraries. Despite this, the school opened and operated for thirteen years (Wiegand, 2017; Wiegand & Wiegand, 2018). ALA did take a stand on segregation in 1936, declaring that all attendees at the annual conference would be allowed in conference rooms regardless of race. However, with one notable exception discussed in the next paragraph, ALA did not take a firm or explicit stance on issues of segregation and library services at the state, regional, or local levels.

In the 1950s, ALA pushed for professional integration by allowing only one official library association per state and requiring that the ALA-affiliated associations "had to admit all members who applied, regardless of race" (Wiegand, 2017, p. 4). Many state associations refused to comply, particularly in the South, and lost their affiliation with ALA. ALA's Intellectual Freedom Committee (IFC) reached out to southern librarians to determine "if an ALA statement supporting library integration would be helpful" (Wiegand, 2017, p. 4); however, librarians said they would not find this to be helpful, either because they supported segregation or were concerned about the trouble it might cause them. Rick Estes (1960), an African American librarian at the Pratt Institute, highlighted ALA's reluctance to truly make a stand in the article "Segregated Libraries." As Wiegand points out, African American citizens' taxes were used to pay for libraries that either denied them service or offered them unequal service, and Estes declared that ALA

> has been completely ineffective about the issue. It
> has never even passed a resolution on the subject.
> It has never commended the efforts of Negro readers and organizations who have tried to end library

> segregation by doing everything from making a
> mild request to staging library sit-ins. It has not
> attempted to bring a law suit [sic] or lent its name
> as *amicus curiae* to any group bringing a suit. (Estes,
> 1960, as cited in Wiegand, 2017, p. 6)

Furthermore, when in 1961 "the US Civil Rights Commission called for congressional action to withhold federal funds under the Library Services Act from states using those funds to maintain segregated library services" (Wiegand, 2017, p. 10), ALA once again failed to take a meaningful stand. Though the board did discuss recommendations for enforcing both the requirement for ALA-affiliated state associations to accept all applicants and to deny membership to libraries whose services were segregated, their ultimate concern was alienating membership—stating that these recommendations would result in "breaches of understanding and professional relations . . . that would require years to heal" (Wiegand, 2017, p. 11)—rather than the deleterious effect on Black and African American communities and library professionals that would take decades or generations to heal. In 2018, almost 60 years after Estes's article, the ALA Council did adopt a resolution acknowledging the harm that segregated libraries caused Black and African American communities, as well as ALA's complicity in perpetuating these harms ("ALA Honors African Americans," 2018).

Although ALA failed to take a firm and direct stance on the desegregation of public libraries in the mid-twentieth century, many fought for Black and African American citizens to have equal library access.[1] The US Commission on Civil Rights published "an investigation into southern libraries" in 1963, reporting that "'two thirds of the Negro population of 13 Southern States were entirely without library services' and that 'nearly 10 million Negro citizens of our land are totally or partially denied access to publicly owned books'" (Selby, 2019, p. 9). The fight started long before that, however. In 1902, W. E. B. DuBois advocated for library services to Black Americans and African Americans in Atlanta, though he was ultimately denied (Knott, 2015). In 1939, attorney Samuel Wilbur Tucker led a read-in at the Alexandria (VA)

BOX 3.1

Description of a Black/African American Branch Library from the Perspective of a Black/African American Newspaper

The following is a reproduction of an article about the Archer Street library branch from the *Tulsa Star* newspaper on March 20, 1920 (p. 7). The *Star*, founded in 1912 by editor and publisher Andrew Jackson Smitherman, "championed African-American causes, promoting progress and stability within Tulsa's black community until its dramatic and untimely demise following the Race Massacre of May 31, 1921" (Oklahoma Historical Society, n.d.). The *Star* was located in the neighborhood called Black Wall Street, which was destroyed by a White mob on May 31, 1921. Between 150 and 200 people were killed in this massacre, and prominent businesses were burned down, including the public library, a dozen churches, five hotels, thirty-one restaurants, four drugstores, and eight doctor offices. Because the *Star* "repeatedly criticized its [the city administration's] actions towards the African-American community," "Smitherman was forced to flee Tulsa when whites blamed him for inciting the 'riot.'" He was indicted, though he was never extradited to stand trial (O'Dell,

n.d.), nor did he return to Tulsa (Tulsa City-County Library, 2018). However, his name was eventually cleared as being wrongfully indicted (Tulsa City-County Library, 2018).

According to the April 3, 1915 edition of the *Tulsa Star*, the Colored Library branch was located in the newspaper's lobby on Archer Street, though articles in the *Star* indicated that it had various locations throughout its existence. It appears that the branch was originally funded by Mr. J. B. Stradford, a prominent resident of the neighborhood. The article states that Mr. Stradford "finally interested Mayor Wooden and thru him the city commissioners were persuaded to give $10.00 a month which paid only for one half of the salary of the librarian Mr. Stradford employed." However, according to the May 8, 1920 edition, "The first official act of the new administration after making appointments, was to discontinue the appropriation for the Colored library for an indefinite period of time." It appears that funding was restored according to the May 22, 1920 edition, though the community was responsible for paying for a

new site for the library and later issues discuss successful fundraisers.

At the time of the March 1920 publication, it appears that the Librarian at the Archer Street library branch is none other than the editor and publisher of the *Tulsa Star*, Andrew Jackson Smitherman, accompanied by his wife as the Assistant Librarian. However, having browsed many issues of the *Star*, it appears that many community members served in the Librarian role, and the Smithermans were not the only librarians who served the community.

The Colored Library branch was destroyed in the Tulsa Race Massacre (or Black Wall Street Massacre) just over a year after the following article was published in the Star. According to the 1921 Tulsa City Directory, the "public library" was located at 429 Archer Street–East. There is no entry for 429 Archer Street–East in the 1922 Directory. This also means that the community most likely never got to build the new library for which they worked so hard to raise funds to pay for the site they had purchased.

From the Tulsa Star, *March 20, 1920*

Librarian Succeeds in Obtaining Additional Consideration on Part of Authorities

The rain storm accompanied by thunder and lightning last Wednesday night indicates that the back of winter is broken, and spring, gentle spring is here, or near any way. And just to think, that day our Colored Librarian had had set up in the reading room of the Colored Library on Archer street, a large and handsome stove capable of radiating its generous heat to the farthermost nooks of

the room. The installation of this new stove was necessary, especially because during all the coldest days of the past winter, the Assistant Librarian, Mrs. A. Smitherman has been up against the problem of trying to keep warm enough to feel she was still alive. The problem of stoves and heating is a matter that confronts the Librarian, and no one else and must come out of the pitiful allowance made to

(continued)

maintain this institution. And that is not all, there is the salary of the Assistant Librarian and many incidental expenses gas, lighting, cleaning and the like, which must be met by the Librarian, and on top of that he is furnishing his own building as quarters for the library for the use of the Colored People of Tulsa. Surely that is a burden for one man to assume and carry on successfully.

Many other Sinbad, carrying such a load, would quite naturally devote considerable time urging a greater allowance, through which he might personally realize relief and benefit. But not so, through the efforts of Mr. A.J. Smitherman, Librarian, the local authorities have been made wise to the primitive conditions found at the Colored Library, as with those provided for the whites at the magnificent public library down town, and as a result of his efforts a greater degree of interest is to be shown and the Colored Library made more attractive, interesting, and suitable as a place for young people to go and read. Among other things in anticipation, it is planned to place on the shelves a full line of the works of Negro authors and popular magazines. There is every reason to believe when the Colored People of Tulsa themselves show wider interest in this institution, that it will soon become one of such character and usefulness, that one and all will take pride in it.

In addition, it may be said Mr. Smitherman, Librarian, has offered the use of the library room free of charge for night meeting purposes by any Tulsa organization interested in Race uplift. —(Hack).

Issues of the Tulsa Star *can be searched and viewed at https://gateway.okhistory.org/explore/collections/ TULSA/.*

Public Library (Knott, 2015; Selby, 2019; Wiegand & Wiegand, 2018). Having been denied a library card, Tucker and five men entered the library, retrieved a book, sat down, and began reading. When the police arrived, the men refused to leave and were arrested. The charges were dismissed, and the Alexandria Public Library did not desegregate for a couple of decades. A similar read-in, though led by high school students, occurred at the Danville (VA) Public Library in 1960 (Knott, 2015; Selby, 2019; Wiegand & Wiegand, 2018). The library attempted to avoid desegregation by closing, but a court ultimately required the library to reopen and desegregate. These library read-ins were prevalent across the South in the 1950s and 1960s (Wiegand & Wiegand, 2018).

Many library read-ins ended peacefully, but that was not always the case, despite the desegregationists' nonviolent tactics. Many faced beatings and arrest for simply requesting a library card to a Whites-only branch, typically a city's main library. For example, in 1963, two pastors—Reverend Nimrod Quintus Reynolds and Reverend Bob McClain—were beaten by members of the Ku Klux Klan when they were fighting for the desegregation of the Anniston, Alabama, public library (Garrison, 2013; Wiegand & Wiegand, 2018). This violence also extended to the establishment of Freedom Libraries, which appeared across southern states, particularly in Mississippi, during the Freedom Summer of 1964 to provide Black and African American citizens access to books, job training, cultural programming, political dialogue, and a place of community (Beasley, 2017; Selby, 2019; Wiegand & Wiegand, 2018). In addition to providing the community with books, many of these libraries also hosted literacy programs, not just for children, but also for adults. Adult literacy programs were necessary because some states had laws that prohibited teaching Black Americans and African Americans basic literacy skills, and in other states their education was denied by social custom (Duster, 2009). Because of this, Freedom Libraries became a site of civic change and empowerment.

In many southern states, Black Americans and African Americans were denied voting rights due to their illiteracy, and the Freedom Library literacy programs were a direct response to this exclusionary tactic. White supremacists did their best to thwart the success of these libraries, including derailing the deliveries of donated materials to the bombing of the buildings (Selby, 2019). In 1964 Micky Schwerner, who helped to set up the Freedom Library and community center in Meridian, Mississippi, was shot and killed by police and Ku Klux Klan members along with James Chaney and Andrew Goodman. As one of our reviewers highlighted, the murder of these three men marked a turning point in the Civil Rights movement, and many who lived during that time or who have studied this era will be familiar with these names. Mickey Schwerner and Andrew Goodman were White Freedom Riders, and their murder caused other White people to take notice, because it was not just Black and African American communities who were being subjected to violence and death in pursuit of equal rights (N. Shabazz, personal communication, March 2, 2021). However, their role in setting up and supporting Freedom Libraries often goes unmentioned. Two years after their murder, in 1966, the Supreme Court established the desegregation of public libraries through the *Brown v. Louisiana* case. Beasley (2017) provides a powerful statement about the desegregation of public libraries:

> The library is a powerful institution in the United States. African Americans' history with this institution is marked by exclusionary laws that prevented access. To transgress the laws risked violence and even death. For African Americans, full admission to the library was an entree to learning, but more significantly, ingress meant being recognized as human, because through learning, self-worth is acknowledged and tactical skills of emancipation are acquired, thus the restoration of one's personhood. (p. 77)

Even after the 1964 Civil Rights Act and the 1966 *Brown v. Louisiana* ruling, many public libraries did what they could to resist integration attempts, including closing facilities to all patrons and repeated appeals of court orders. Once officially integrated, many libraries did not publicly announce this change and some practiced "vertical integration," in which the furniture was removed to discourage members of different races from spending too much time together in library spaces (Wiegand & Wiegand, 2018). Some libraries imposed membership restrictions, in which community members seeking to obtain a library card had to fill out an application that might require them

to provide references. All of these were attempts to discourage Black and African American citizens from using what had historically been the White branches of the public libraries.

Much of the scholarship about public libraries and race, particularly during the twentieth century, has focused primarily on the South and border states (e.g., Oklahoma, West Virginia, Kentucky), as Jim Crow laws and social practices that explicitly segregated races were prevalent in those regions. However, it is important to state that racial discrimination in public libraries was not confined to these regions. Racial discrimination was, in many ways, more covert in other regions of the United States. Wiegand and Wiegand (2018) write that "the discrimination in public library history was enforced by real estate redlining supported by local politicians. These efforts isolated urban public library branches serving black populations" (p. 15). While Black and African American community members had access to all branches of a public library system in theory, in practice neighborhood libraries might have created both separate and unequal experiences based on race. The effects of redlining practices, which enforced racial discrimination within real estate transactions, and racial segregation are also important for understanding race and public education in the United States and are discussed in the next chapter.

THE CONTEMPORARY CONTEXT

Over the past two decades, more scholarly attention has been paid to racism and the history of public libraries in the United States. However, scholarship and publications about Black and African American communities' relationship(s) with and use of public libraries since the Civil Rights era remain scant. We discovered only a few publications that directly, tangentially, or superficially discuss Black and African American users or communities and their public library experiences. A 2015 Pew Research Center report addressed race and public library usage and disaggregated data among racial groups, as opposed to simply discussing race in terms of White and non-White (Horrigan, 2015). Black Americans and

African Americans were more likely to ask for help from a librarian and use computers or the internet at libraries, but they were less likely to borrow books. In addition, they were more likely to believe that libraries are important for employment-seeking activities, including entrepreneurship, and that losing their public library "would have a major impact on them and their family" (Horrigan, 2015, p. 9). Despite this, library usage declined for African Americans between 2012 and 2015.

Some of this decline in usage might be due to the racial climate of public libraries. Giulietti et al. (2019) conducted an e-mail correspondence study with local public agencies, including public libraries, across the United States to determine if discrimination based on the perceived race of the sender was evident. They sent almost 20,000 basic e-mail inquiries, inquiries that would not require an in-depth response from these public agencies, using sender names that would most likely be considered Black or African American (DeShawn Jackson and Tyrone Washington) or White (Jake Mueller and Greg Walsh). The response rate for the entire sample was just under 70 percent, though the difference in the response rates was almost 4 percent lower for the African American senders, and the African American senders were less likely to receive a response with a cordial tone. The difference in the response rate for public libraries was statistically significant. The authors ran models with two different approaches to determine if the likely race of the recipient/responder affects the responses and found that African American senders were more likely to receive a response from agencies in areas in which the recipient/responder was more likely to be Black or African American. This finding suggests that implicit or explicit bias likely influences if and how White employees respond to users who are perceived to be Black or African American, and that Black and African American users are more likely to receive a response from Black or African American employees.

Several studies about youth and their relationship to their public libraries either directly or indirectly highlight the experiences of Black and African American users. Agosto and Hughes-Hassell (2005) explored the information-seeking behaviors of 27 urban teenagers, 25 of whom were African American. The students were either enrolled in an after-school program through the Boys and Girls Club or were part of a leadership program at the public library. In interviews with the Boys and Girls Club students, the students viewed the public library as being "dirty, unwelcoming, and unexciting" (Hughes-Hassell, 2005, p. 151). Although the leadership students were employed by the library, they did not view librarians as being a helpful source of information. Students in both groups rarely used their public library. Some students perceived that the public library had services and programming for children and adults, but nothing targeting teens. Other students indicated that they had previously had bad experiences with library staff, including when they were looking for books they wanted to read. The students expressed that library staff tended to be rude to teens, and they did not feel that the library had culturally relevant materials in their collections.

Several studies have explored reading habits, participation in reading programs, and access to reading material of Black and African American and urban youth. Celano and Neuman (2001) conducted a study based on summer reading program participation in public libraries and at day camps, and the children who participated were primarily African American. Although they found positive implications for the literacy levels of the children who participated in the public library programs, race was not explored in the published analysis. In a study of urban middle schoolers' leisure reading habits, Hughes-Hassell and Lutz (2006) found that public librarians were quite low on the list of people who encouraged the students to read. Kumasi (2008) documented the experiences of 13 African American students who participated in a culturally responsive book club at a public library. She found that participation in this club influenced the racial identity development of the students, both through confronting Whiteness and through giving voice to their own experiences. Evans (2019) documents the experiences of three teens—two of whom are Black—who participated in a book club run by a White librarian. Her study indicates how the librarian's genuine and supportive engagement in the interests of these teens helped to nurture the teens' love of reading. Neuman and Moland (2019) examined the availability of reading materials for purchase in low-income neighborhoods in three cities, declaring them book deserts in terms of children's books. They note that public libraries are likely the only source of children's books in these neighborhoods, yet they cite previous research using a national survey indicating that only 8 percent of residents of low-income neighborhoods use their public libraries (Rideout & Katz, 2016, as cited in Neuman & Moland, 2019).

A few publications are tangentially related to public libraries and Black/African American users or communities. Several studies that investigated public library usage, funding, and benefits based on neighborhood include discussions of the racial characteristics (Gong et al., 2008; Johnson, 2010; Sin, 2011). However, in most cases, these studies do not analyze the data by race to highlight specific needs of Black and African American users or communities, though these can possibly be inferred. Spink and Cole (2001) surveyed residents at a community housing project in Dallas, Texas, the overwhelming majority of whom were African American, to learn more about their information-seeking behavior. They found that the majority of the participants (two-thirds) did not regularly use public libraries. This lack of usage might be attributed to the lack of political power afforded to communities of color, which affects residents' ability to advocate for resources, including how money allocated to their communities is spent by elected officials, public servants, and developers (Gong et al., 2008). In addition, communities of color, particularly those that are lower income, face other more pressing issues, such as personal safety, deteriorating housing, and lack of access to nutritious foods (Gong et al., 2008; Overbey, 2020; Spink & Cole, 2001). This is in stark contrast to middle-class and upper-class neighborhoods, which tend to be Whiter, often have political power, and do not face the same day-to-day challenges of survival.

When residents of low-income communities do use their library, their experiences are likely different from those of people who live in wealthier neighborhoods. Even in higher-income communities, Black and

African Americans' experiences using libraries may differ from those of their White peers. Robinson (2019) discusses the increase in security and policing in North American public libraries and highlights how LIS literature has been uncritical of the detrimental effect that this might have for BIPOC users and other marginalized and stigmatized user populations, including those who suffer from mental illness, are experiencing homelessness, have developmental disabilities, or struggle with addiction. Given the antagonistic and often violent relationship that many law enforcement agencies have historically had and currently have with Black and African American communities, the presence of security in the public library can be perceived as threatening and may reinforce feelings of constant surveillance and monitoring. This is an issue that will be revisited regarding public schools in the next chapter.

Much like the Freedom Libraries in the summer of 1964, some public libraries have become places of refuge for their communities during times of turmoil (Beasley, 2017; Chancellor, 2017), particularly during protests related to the murder of Black citizens by law enforcement. Well-known examples include the Ferguson Municipal Public Library in Ferguson, Missouri, and the Pennsylvania Avenue branch of the Enoch Pratt Free Library in Baltimore, Maryland. Both Beasley (2017) and Chancellor (2017) provide overviews of the services these libraries offered and the role they played within their communities as they experienced turmoil and crisis that was being showcased on a national level. The decisions made by these public libraries (and others) who serve predominantly Black and African American communities during these times of crisis is noteworthy, as it eschews the idea that libraries are neutral spaces (Gibson et al., 2017). Furthermore, many public libraries have demonstrated a serious commitment to racial equity in their service provision. The Government Alliance on Race and Equity (GARE) has worked with public libraries throughout the country to apply their racial equity framework to make real change in the ways that the libraries operate and serve their communities (Sonnie, 2018). Gibson et al. (2017) discuss how the idea of libraries as neutral spaces has allowed libraries to uphold status quo (i.e., White supremacy) by ignoring or disengaging with potentially controversial political and social issues, much like ALA's failure to meaningfully engage with the (de)segregation in the middle of the twentieth century. Furthermore, many public libraries have demonstrated a serious commitment to racial equity in their service provision.

CONCLUSION

Much progress has been made in terms of racial inclusion since the founding of public libraries in the United States. When public libraries first started to appear, many communities either excluded their Black and African American residents altogether or provided them with separate and unequal resources and facilities. This means that public libraries historically were designed to serve only a particular segment of the overall population. While all libraries across the country have now been integrated in theory, in practice residential segregation is quite normal in this country and could result in segregated library systems or branch libraries with inequities in funding, resources, and facilities. Furthermore, the LIS profession continues to remain overwhelmingly White, meaning that many libraries might still operate in ways that continue to serve White patrons but marginalize BIPOC communities. The fact that Black and African American usage of public libraries has declined in recent years might be indicative of a need to reimagine what inclusive public libraries should be. However, many public libraries across the country are doing this work (Sonnie, 2018), so there is hope that this reimagination will become more widespread.

There remains a noticeable lack of discoverable scholarship, research, assessment, and program evaluation regarding Black and African American communities' public library experiences and usage, which means that we do not know if and how our resources, services, spaces, and programming are adequately meeting their needs.[2] This is troubling due to the racialized history of public libraries and the fact that desegregation of our public libraries happened relatively recently. When there is absence of race-centered, equity-minded scholarship and research, then we often use assumptions to guide our decision making and practice. Again, given the demographics of the profession overall, this is dangerous, as assumptions are often based on one's lived experience and reflect both implicit and explicit biases. For example, if we do not seek to understand the decline in library usage of Black and African American communities at local, regional, and national levels, then we might attribute this decline to mythical cultural deficit narratives that are common with color evasiveness (Bonilla-Silva, 2018; Burke, 2019). Assumptions based on these cultural deficit narratives might lead one to conclude that particular communities are not interested in reading, learning, or education, rather than considering that library hours or policies, gaps in collections or resources, or a lack of targeted outreach about what the library has to offer could be significant barriers to usage.

The research that does exist indicates that Black and African American communities value their public libraries (Beasley, 2017; Gibson et al., 2017; Horrigan, 2015), might be less likely to receive a response to their inquiries (Giulietti et al., 2019), feel like there are not culturally relevant resources (Agosto & Hughes-Hassell, 2005), and perceive library staff as being unapproachable (Agosto & Hughes-Hassell, 2005). On the other hand, some research has found that culturally relevant programming coupled with genuine care on behalf of the librarian has a positive impact on young Black and African American library users (Evans, 2019; Kumasi, 2008). The findings that we share in *Narratives of (Dis)Engagement* indicate that learning and literacy are important to our students' families, and the students regularly use their public libraries to feed their need to read. However, in many cases, library staff did not proactively engage many of these students, which means the students were often unaware of library programming beyond summer reading programs. There are obvious limitations to the generalizability of this existing research to all public libraries across the country; however, these studies provide a foundation for future exploration to understand how public libraries can engage, support, and serve their Black and African American users and communities.

RECOMMENDED READING

Battles, D. M. (2009). *The history of public library access for African Americans in the South: Or, leaving behind the plow.* Scarecrow Press.

Eberhart, G. M. (2018, June 25). Desegregating public libraries: The untold story of civil rights heroes in the Jim Crow South. *American Libraries.* https://americanlibrariesmagazine.org/blogs/the-scoop/desegregating-public-libraries/

Fultz, M. (2006). Black public libraries in the South in the era of de jure segregation. *Libraries and the Cultural Record*, 41(3), 337–359.

Gibson, A. N., Chancellor, R. L., Cooke, N. A., Dahlen, S. P., Lee, S. A., & Shorish, Y. L. (2017). Libraries on the frontlines: Neutrality and social justice. *Equality, Diversity and Inclusion*, 36(8), 751–766.

Granville County Library System. (n.d.). *The heroes of desegregating in public libraries.* https://granville.lib.nc.us/2019/02/the-heroes-of-desegregating-in-public-libraries/

Holloway, K. F. C. (2006). *BookMarks: Reading in black and white.* Rutgers University Press.

Honma, T. (2005). Trippin' over the color line: The invisibility of race in library and information studies. *InterActions: UCLA Journal of Education and Information Studies*, 1(2), n.p.

Jones, P. A. (2004). *Still struggling for equality: Public library services with minorities.* Libraries Unlimited.

Knott, C. (2015). *Not free, not for all: Public libraries in the age of Jim Crow.* University of Massachusetts Press.

Selby, M. (2019). *Freedom libraries: The untold story of libraries for African Americans in the South.* Rowman & Littlefield.

Wiegand, W. A. (2017). Any ideas? The American Library Association and the desegregation of public libraries in the American South. *Libraries: Culture, History, and Society*, 1(1), 1–22.

Wiegand, W. A., & Wiegand, S. A. (2018). *The desegregation of public libraries in the Jim Crow South: Civil rights and local activism.* Louisiana State University Press.

NOTES

1. Many brave individuals fought for the desegregation of public libraries. For sources that provide more information about these individuals, please see this chapter's Recommended Reading list.

2. It is important to acknowledge that there are likely public libraries who are doing race-centered assessment and program evaluation, which often remains internal to the library or to the community it serves. However, this work, even when posted publicly, is not easy to discover. This is significant because the profession overall could benefit from easy access to the race-centered assessment and evaluation that public libraries are doing.

4

SCHOOL LIBRARIES

OVERVIEW

The differences in educational outcomes, including grades, test scores, and graduation rates, of students of various racial backgrounds in public K–12 education in the United States have been highly publicized for several decades. While many commentators and administrators attempt to make sense of these persistent disparities and why they persist, the historical and generational trauma from being denied a quality education is rarely discussed. As we discuss in this chapter, this inequitable legacy survives in the form of differential funding and resources provided to minority-majority schools. Furthermore, race, as a social construct, affects the ways in which students are treated within educational institutions, including who is perceived as a good student and worthy of a teacher's investment. In this chapter, we provide a brief exploration of the racialized history and practices within public K–12 education in the United States, including a discussion of relevant LIS research. We believe it is important to consider school libraries within the broader context of K–12 public education to gain a holistic view of Black and African American students' collective experiences with schooling. Indeed, Virginia Lacy Jones, who was the dean of the School of Library Service at Atlanta University (presently Clark Atlanta University) for almost 40 years, wrote in her 1945 dissertation that "school library service and problems cannot be considered separately from the programs and problems of the school; thus, there must be an understanding of the framework in which the school and library operate" (Jones, 1945, p. 187, as cited in Fultz, 2006, p. 337).

THE BROADER K-12 PUBLIC SCHOOL CONTEXT IN THE UNITED STATES

In many ways, the history of public education and race mirrors the history of public libraries and race. This is not terribly surprising given that both public libraries and educational institutions are at the very core of our democracy and have complementary goals. Indeed, similar to the development of public libraries in the United States, one of the initial purposes of public education was that of assimilation to White cultural values (Noguera, 2008). However, in both cases, the fact that Black and African American people were not initially considered full citizens of the United States is quite apparent. Black and African American people were historically excluded from both institutions, both by law (de jure) and by societal practice (de facto). The ability to freely access information and build knowledge determines who the democracy believes is legitimate or deserving of citizenship. We believe it is important to have this contextual and historical foundation so we can critically analyze the current and future implications of America's apartheid past.

Many readers are likely more familiar with the prevalence of segregated public schools, particularly in the Jim Crow South, and the fight to desegregate them than with the history of segregated public libraries that we shared in the previous chapter. Public school segregation was not just a problem of the Jim Crow South, however. Other regions of the United States also maintained segregated schools both before and after the 1954 *Brown v. Board of Education* Supreme Court ruling. Although some states did have laws that required or allowed segregation through the early 1950s, much of the educational segregation in other regions of the country was a result of segregated housing practices (Clotfelter, 2004). Restrictive covenants, or "the insertion into deeds the promise not to sell a property to blacks or members of other specified groups" (Clotfelter, 2004, p. 19), are one example of how Black and African American citizens were excluded from living in certain areas. Although these were "declared unenforceable in 1948" (Clotfelter, 2004, p. 19), they set the foundation for other strategies to segregate cities and neighborhoods by race. Redlining, which relates to the determination of which homes were able to obtain a mortgage and/or insurance, was another common tactic used in the twentieth century to ensure that White neighborhoods remained White (Grant, 2011). The practice that resulted in racist redlining was initially meant to help homeowners keep their homes during the Great Depression. Maps were color coded to identify which neighborhoods were at most risk of defaulting on mortgages and based on perceived security risks. Wealthier White neighborhoods were typically coded green, and neighborhoods with Jewish residents typically received a blue status. Red was assigned to neighborhoods "even if only one black family resided there, on the assumption that it would soon be all-black and 'undesirable' or even 'hazardous'" (Grant, 2011, p. 16). Redlining was still practiced as late as the

1970s.[1] Other practices that resulted in racially segregated schools included gerrymandering school zones and district lines, creating small school districts, selectively locating housing projects in particular neighborhoods, and white flight from cities to suburban neighborhoods (Clotfelter, 2004).

Despite the significance of the landmark *Brown v. Board of Education* Supreme Court decision in 1954, schools across the United States remained segregated. In addition to strong resistance from the southern states, the Brown decision was "lacking any reference to enforcement" (Clotfelter, 2004, p. 13). Due to lack of action, the Supreme Court issued *Brown II* in 1955, indicating that the 1954 *Brown* ruling that supported desegregation should be followed with "all deliberate speed." Again, this was not just a southern problem. In the early 1960s, the NAACP took legal action against more than 50 school districts in regions other than the South that remained racially segregated. It was not until the mid-1960s, through a series of legislation and subsequent Supreme Court decisions, that desegregation became enforceable. The Civil Rights Act was passed in 1964 and was quickly followed by the Elementary and Secondary Education Act of 1965, the latter of which attached federal funding to desegregation efforts. Some cities interpreted *Brown* to mean that they could no longer promote school segregation but not that they needed to actively move toward integration. In 1968 the Supreme Court clarified the definition of desegregation as "the abolition of identifiably white and black schools" (Clotfelter, 2004, p. 26) through the *Green v. County School Board of New Kent County* decision. In 1971 the Supreme Court ruled that the *Brown* decision also applied to school districts that were racially segregated as a result of residential segregation, thus ordering "remedies where residential segregation had made segregation in the public schools almost inevitable" (Clotfelter, 2004, p. 27). Although progress was made in integrating public schools, the composition of the Supreme Court changed in the early 1970s under President Nixon. School (de)segregation was on his mind as he considered whom he would nominate. Nixon said, "I don't care if he's a Democrat or Republican. Third, within the definition of conservative, he must be against busing, and against forced housing integration. Beyond that, he can do what he pleases" (Clotfelter, 2004, p. 31). A few years later, the Supreme Court issued an important ruling in the *Milliken v. Bradley* case, in that "no desegregation remedy could be extended beyond a single school district" (Clotfelter, 2004, p. 31). This meant that school districts that had been created based on gerrymandering or neighborhood boundaries would not be forced to remedy the resultant racial segregation. This decision has significant implications for the present racial composition of public schools in the United States.

The United States is more racially and ethnically diverse now than ever, and we are moving toward becoming a minority-majority country. In terms of public education, the National Center for Education Statistics (NCES, 2021b) reports that of overall public school enrollments, the proportion of White students significantly dropped between 2009 and 2018—from 54 to 47 percent. There was a small decrease in the percentage of Black/African American students during that same period—from 17 to 15 percent. The majority of the change was due to an increase in Hispanic/Latinx students—from 22 to 27 percent. Because of these changing demographics, one might assume that de facto racial segregation in schools will decrease over time. However, recent NCES statistics show that racial and ethnic school segregation is increasing. NCES (2019a) reports that the percentage of Black/African American students who attended minority-majority schools (i.e., schools with 75 percent or more of their population being racial or ethnic minorities) increased between 2000 and 2015—from 51 to 58 percent. The percentage of White students attending minority-majority schools slightly increased—from 3 to 5 percent—though the overall number is negligible. In 2015 just over 51 percent of White students were enrolled in public elementary and secondary schools "where the combined enrollment [of] minority students was 25 percent or less of total enrollment" (NCES, 2019a, para. 4).

Residential and school segregation both have significant implications for school funding. This is partially due to the reliance on property taxes to fund schools (Camera, 2019). Wealthier neighborhoods often have higher property taxes than lower-income neighborhoods, thus generating more available funding before state or federal provisions are taken into account. Reporting on recent research by EdBuild (2019), *U.S. News and World Report* noted, "school districts where the majority of students enrolled are students of color receive $23 *billion* [emphasis added] less in education funding than predominantly white school districts, despite serving the same number of students" (Camera, 2019, para. 1). In addition, "on average, poor nonwhite school districts receive 19 percent, or about $2,600, less *per student* [emphasis added] than affluent white school districts" (Camera, 2019, para. 8), though this disparity was much greater in some states, including Arizona and Oklahoma. Even when comparing poor diverse districts and poor White districts the disparity remained, with an 11 percent ($1,500 per student) difference in funding, on average. The CEO of EdBuild, Rebecca Sibilia, believes this "hammers home the deep roots of racial inequality in education funding" (Camera, 2019, para. 13). For many students, the difference in funding and resources likely leads to a both separate and unequal experience, despite the fact that segregation of public institutions has been illegal for decades.

Black and African American students might face segregation even within schools that are relatively well integrated in terms of race. There are several ways in which students are sorted into different academic tracks within schools based on their perceived abilities (Pirtle, 2019). Noguera (2008) highlights the importance of this sorting for both the short term and the long term in that children "develop expectations regarding where they will end up on the social hierarchy" (p. 118). Despite comprising 15 percent of public school enrollment, only 9 percent of students in gifted education programs are Black/African American (Dreilinger, 2020). Dreilinger (2020) points out the racial roots of gifted education—the psychologist who helped to popularize the intelligence quotient (IQ), Lewis Terman, was an avowed eugenicist. Black and Latinx students are underrepresented within gifted education as a result of "teacher underreferal, test bias and unfairness, and discriminatory policies and procedures" (Ford, 2013, p. 62). Furthermore, Black/

African American students are less likely to be enrolled in advanced courses, such as Advanced Placement (AP), International Baccalaureate (IB), and dual enrollment courses, than their White peers—30 percent versus 44 percent—despite the availability of these courses being the same, on average (National Center for Education Statistics, 2019f). Black and Latino students have the least amount of access to AP and gifted education classes (Ford, 2006).

Black and African American students are overrepresented in special education and remedial education classes, although this claim has been empirically contested. Fish (2019) provides a significant contribution to understanding the representation of Black and African American students in special education, as well as an overview of this empirical contestation. Raw numbers, such as basic frequency distributions, often indicate that Black and African American students represent a higher proportion of special education students than do White students. For example, in Fish's study using data from the Wisconsin Department of Instruction from 2010–11, the proportion of Black and African American students in special education was nearly double that of White students. Furthermore, when basic predictive models that take race and gender into account have been used, the findings have further confirmed that Black and African American students are more likely to be sorted into special education. However, when more complex predictive models that account for other variables such as socioeconomic status have been used, the relationship between race and special education disappears and socioeconomic status becomes a significant predictor, though there is a relationship between race and socioeconomic status in the United States. Fish found that race becomes an important predictor when running even more complex predictive models, ones that account for both school racial composition and the social stigma associated with the particular disability, including the resources and support that are normally provided. For higher-status disabilities, which include attention-deficit/hyperactivity disorder (ADHD), speech-language impairment, and autism spectrum disorder, White students are more likely to be placed into special education in schools that have higher proportions of students of color. For lower-status disabilities, which include emotional disturbance and intellectual disability, students of color, including Black and African American students, are more likely to be sorted into special education in schools where the proportion of White students is higher. This has important implications for within-school segregation because students with lower-status disabilities are more likely to be isolated from their grade-level peers while students with higher-status disabilities are more likely to receive accommodations that allow them to remain in many classes with their grade-level peers. Fish states that the inequality of categorization "both [creates] and [reinforces] racialized categories of disability and [reinforces] racial inequality" (Fish, 2019, p. 2595). Others, such as Johnson (2013), argue that Black children are misdiagnosed due to cultural and language barriers, as well as racist practices, which could be mitigated by the adoption of culturally responsive pedagogical practices.

In addition to injurious academic tracking and sorting to which many Black and African American students are subjected, they are also more likely to be disciplined and punished than their White peers, which for some students creates a school-to-prison pipeline. Based on 2015–16 data from the Civil Rights Data Collection, Riddle and Sinclair (2019) report the disparities in discipline between White students and Black and African American students. Black and African American students were almost three times more likely to face in-school suspension, more than four times as likely to face out-of-school suspension, more than two times as likely to be expelled, almost three times as likely to face a law enforcement referral, and three times as likely to face school arrest. These statistics are troublingly similar to incarceration rates for Black and African American citizens in the United States. Black Americans and African Americans comprise 13 percent of US residents but 40 percent of incarcerated populations (Prison Policy Initiative, 2020). Furthermore, Black and African American youth are more than two times as likely to be arrested and four times as likely to be committed to a detention center than their White peers, despite similarities in the likelihood that Black and White youth will engage in activities that could lead to arrest or detention (Sentencing Project, 2016).

Likely compounding this issue is the increasing presence of law enforcement in public schools in the United States. Based on 2017–18 data from NCES, just under half of public schools had either a full-time or part-time school resource officer, 13 percent had other kinds of law enforcement present, and another 22 percent had security personnel (Diliberti et al., 2019). Mbekeani-Wiley (2017) reports that "school-based policing is the fastest growing area of law enforcement" (p. 6), and the presence of law enforcement in schools "increases the likelihood that a student will be referred to law enforcement for adolescent behavior" (p. 4), particularly for students of color. In Denver, for example, Black students comprise 13 percent of the students in the school district but accounted for 29 percent of law enforcement referrals in 2018–19 (Camera, 2020). Furthermore, Camera (2020) reports, "from 2014 to 2019, there were 4,540 police tickets and arrests within Denver schools—87% of them students of color" (para. 4). Zero-tolerance policies further compound this issue, especially since they often exist in tandem with law enforcement in schools (Heitzig, 2009). These policies can be heavy-handed and harsh, often not taking into account contextual information. Noguera (2008) provides an example of a student with an "exemplary academic record" (p. 98) who brought a loaded handgun to school because his father was suicidal and asked the student to remove it from the home. He had not shown the gun to anyone, but he talked to a friend about it because he was not sure what he should do. Despite hearing the full account of the event and the student's high performance in school, the board ultimately decided to expel the student because of the zero-tolerance policy.

Just as Mbekeani-Wiley (2017) indicated that students were being referred for discipline for "adolescent behavior," students feel that these referrals are for trivial matters and are unfair. Students in Ray's (2015) study about African American students and school discipline in the Los Angeles area reported that "being tardy to class, talking, or not doing their work" (p. x) often resulted in a referral to the office rather than being handled in the classroom. Furthermore,

these students reported that teachers made assumptions about student behavior and acted on those assumptions, rather than speaking to the student to determine what was actually happening. Examples provided include the assumption that a student was texting when he was actually looking for a pencil in his backpack and that students who were talking were doing so inappropriately rather than discussing their schoolwork. Indeed, Noguera (2008) writes, "the factors that give rise to misbehavior go unexplored, ignored, and unaddressed, while the penchant to punish proceeds with little thought given to the long-term consequences on students" (p. 121).

Despite the prevalence of heavy-handed discipline and school policing, there is no evidence that these tactics are actually effective (Heitzig, 2009; Noguera, 2008). Quite the opposite. First, Noguera (2008) points out the irony in consistently removing students of color from instruction time, especially since the previous research covered in this chapter highlights persistent equity gaps in educational outcomes. Furthermore, this kind of punishment is effective only if the students who are being punished find school and instruction time to be valuable, but schools have often demonstrated to these students that they do not belong or that they are not worthy of investment through racialized sorting and tracking and inequitable funding. There are also consequences for the entire school population, as law enforcement presence, including metal detectors, requires funding to sustain, often at the expense of academic or "educational programs and services" (Noguera, 2008, p. 87). This includes laying off "counselors, nurses, social workers, and scores of teachers" to maintain police presence in schools" (Burnette, 2020, para. 1). Finally, for many students of color, the constant presence of and surveillance by law enforcement in their schools can be traumatic, due to racialized policing practices in the United States, including the frequent murders of unarmed Black and African American citizens (Camera, 2020). Although more schools are choosing to defund their relationships with law enforcement, heavy-handed discipline and consistent school law enforcement referrals create a pipeline into the larger criminal justice system in the United States, including the mass incarceration of Black and African American citizens.

One potential contributing factor to both sorting and punishment is teachers' perceptions of the abilities of their students because teachers often make significant decisions or play important roles that affect these processes (Fish, 2017; Noguera, 2008). Several recent studies have found that teachers have different expectations and perceptions of students' academic abilities based on race (Fish, 2017; Gershenson et al., 2016; Irizarry & Cohen, 2019). Furthermore, Riddle and Sinclair (2019) found a correlation between county-level racial bias and racialized differences in school discipline, indicating that teachers' implicit or explicit biases likely account for the differential treatment of Black and African American students. Irizarry and Cohen (2019) provide an excellent overview of previous research that explores the relationship between students' race and teacher perceptions, including the implications for students' educational outcomes. They write that, particularly for marginalized student populations, when students perceive that teachers hold a positive perception of them, this is "associated with increased effort and engagement in the classroom, greater school attachment, higher academic achievement, and more positive emotional development" (Irizarry & Cohen, 2019, p. 94), all of which have consequences for students' current and future educational outcomes. However, existing research, including the recent research cited here, has found that teachers tend to have lower expectations and perceptions of Black and African American students' abilities and negative perceptions of this student population's behavior, motivation, and attitude toward schooling.

Furthermore, Black and African American students are less likely to have highly trained teachers in their schools, as teachers with the least amount of experience and credentials tend to work in schools with higher concentrations of students of color (Ford, 2006; Kozol, 2005; Noguera, 2008; Orfield & Lee, 2004). Furthermore, Black and African American students are more likely to experience teacher absenteeism (Miller, 2012), and they are overrepresented in terms of student chronic absenteeism, though the effects are

mitigated when other factors, such as free and reduced-price lunch participation, are considered (Ford & Triplett, 2019). Students who are in minority-majority schools are more likely to have larger class sizes (Barton & Coley, 2009), despite the fact that smaller class sizes have the most positive impact for Black and African American students (Shin, 2012). All of these factors are likely related to disparities in school funding, racialized sorting and tracking practices, and the policing of Black and African American students in schools, as previously discussed.

The ways in which Black and African/African American history is taught in schools are also problematic, as is the whitewashing of this history. Though there have been numerous calls for change, curricula at many schools segregate Black history as something distinct from American history, which can further disenfranchise Black and African American students, indicating that they do not belong or that their identities are not valued. Indeed, James Baldwin suggested these outcomes when speaking before Congress in 1968 (Zimmerman, 2020). Examples of this include a narrow focus on only certain aspects of African history (e.g., Egyptian history) or teaching students only about enslavement or the Civil Rights movement or confining these topics to ethnic studies courses, rather than infusing Black and African American history throughout the curriculum, or focusing on Black and African American history during the month of February—Black History Month (also the shortest month of the year)—rather than throughout the year (Akua, 2015; King, 2016; Mercer, 2020).

Though many educators are realizing the shortcomings of such a reductive curriculum, for all students, not just Black and African American students (Anderson, 2019), as well as the importance of culturally relevant pedagogy (Ladson-Billings, 1995), there remains evidence of continued whitewashing of curricula and textbooks throughout the United States. For example, one Texas history textbook from publisher McGraw-Hill refers to enslaved African Americans as "workers," which suggests that their labor was voluntary and perhaps paid (Isensee, 2015). Adding insult to injury, the same textbook points out that some European immigrants were brought to the

United States as indentured servants. Even more recently, former President Trump convened a commission that would focus on "patriotic education" and a "pro-American curriculum" (Wise, 2020, para. 1). This was in direct response to the increase in curricula that include discussions of systemic racism, with Trump stating that it was perpetuating a "twisted web of lies" and is a "form of child abuse" (Wise, 2020, para. 2). Trump was voted out of office before this commission had time to enact change, though the rhetoric he used is not only injurious—it represents the beliefs of a troubling and not insignificant proportion of the White population in the United States. Many state governments, including the authors' home state of Ohio, are developing legislation that would directly affect the ways in which systemic racism is discussed and taught in public schools.

SCHOOL LIBRARIES LITERATURE

In a recent article, Wiegand (2021) highlights that there were investigations of school libraries as they relate to Black and African American students in the middle of the twentieth century. However, most of these were conducted by Black and African American library school students studying under Virginia Lacy Jones at the historically Black Atlanta University (now Clark Atlanta University). Wiegand writes that Dean Jones "encouraged many of her master's degree students to survey black libraries of all types against the standards that each sector of the library profession had crafted and revised over the decades" (Wiegand, 2021, p. 256). However, at the professional association level, challenges to racist practices and segregation were nonexistent. The American Association of School Librarians (AASL) was even more silent on these issues than ALA. Furthermore, Wiegand discusses how Black school librarians were often relocated to White schools as "a pretense of a satisfactory means to integrate schools" after the *Brown v. Board of Education* decision (Robinson, 1970, p. 281, as cited in Wiegand, 2021, p. 257), which also left Black schools without a librarian.

We identified only one contemporary empirical study that explicitly examined the school library usage and experiences of Black and African American students (Brown, 2007), and another study that did so indirectly (Agosto & Hughes-Hassell, 2005). Using a variety of qualitative data collection methods, Brown (2007) explored the school library experiences, with a focus on computer usage, of a diverse group of 13 students at a large, urban high school. The two library media specialists at the high school were White women. Brown directly addresses several race-related issues in the findings, including the decision to block several ethnicity-oriented websites. Furthermore, Black males seemed to be subjected to a lot of monitoring when using the computers, with Brown noting that many of them would be kicked off computers for playing video games or looking at sneaker or car websites. The library media specialists denied this, though several participants independently corroborated this. One student, Malik, was using a car website for an English project, but he was kicked off the computer before he had a chance to explain that he was using it for academic purposes. He believed that the library media specialists "perceived him as a 'bad kid, ignorant, probably a gang banger'" (Brown, 2007, p. 16), and that perception likely led the librarian to make assumptions about Malik's motives rather than engaging him in a conversation that could have supported his academic needs. Ultimately Brown concludes, "the middle-aged, White female library staff members both extended and restricted students' access to particular ICT-mediated content and activities based on their own perceptions about what was of value and/or appropriate for the school context" (Brown, 2007, p. 19). Although the research site was a public library, Agosto and Hughes-Hassell's (2005) study of the information-seeking behavior of urban youth, the overwhelming majority of whom were Black and African American, is also relevant. The students overall did not have positive impressions of librarians, though some of the students viewed "the school library as a refuge from the unpleasantness of school life" (Agosto & Hughes-Hassell, 2005, p. 151). However, the students felt that their libraries, both public and school, did not have culturally relevant materials in their collections.

Research has demonstrated the importance of well-resourced and well-staffed school libraries to student outcomes and achievement, including for BIPOC students. Lance and Kachel (2018) provide a concise overview of research, which they refer to as school library impact studies, exploring the relationship between school library resources and student performance on standardized reading, writing, and math tests. A study from Pennsylvania found that Black and African American students, in particular, benefit from having a full-time librarian, in that 5.2 percent fewer Black and African American students "tested at the Below Basic level in reading when they had full-time librarians [compared to] those who did not" (Lance & Kachel, 2018, p. 16). In addition, "Black and Latino students whose schools had larger library collections (versus those who did not) more than doubled their percentage of Advanced writing scores and cut their risk of Below Basic writing scores in half" (Lance & Kachel, 2018, p. 16). A study that examined school library quality in the state of Washington found that "a key factor distinguishing high-performing high-poverty schools from low-performing high-poverty schools is a quality library program" (Coker, 2015, p. 25). However, previous research indicates that students in schools with higher concentrations of poverty lack the resources that result in these positive outcomes (Pribesh et al., 2011). All of the differences that Pribesh et al. (2011) found between higher- and lower-poverty schools, based on student eligibility for the free and reduced-price lunch program, were statistically significant. Libraries in schools with higher concentrations of students in poverty were less likely to have more than one full-time librarian, had fewer hours of library availability, added fewer new volumes per year, had a fixed schedule for the library, and had more days closed per year. They conclude that students attending schools with higher concentrations of poverty do not have school library access equal to that of their peers at schools with lower levels of poverty.

Although race has not been an explicit focus, with one exception, literacy research by and for librarians is a topic where race is apparent. Hughes-Hassell and Lutz (2006) explored the leisure reading habits of middle school students at a predominantly Black, urban middle school. Although the analysis was not broken down by race, the demographics of the school suggest that findings likely provide some insight into Black and African American students' habits and attitudes. Most of the students (73 percent) said that they read for leisure, but only 37 percent said they enjoy reading. Not quite half indicated that they thought reading was helpful for their learning. The people who encourage their reading include parents (80 percent), teachers (66 percent), school librarians (29 percent), siblings (25 percent), friends (23 percent), and public librarians (17 percent). The school library was the primary source of reading materials for boys. Kumasi (2008) directly explored race in a study about 13 African American students' participation in a culturally relevant book club at a public library. She found that participation helped the students with their racial identity formation. In 2012 the library community convened a multiday summit to identify strategies for advancing literacy for Black males (Hughes-Hassell et al., 2012).

Related research has investigated the availability of reading materials for youth, as well as their relevance to youth of color. Neuman and Moland (2019) examined the availability of reading materials for purchase in high-poverty and borderline neighborhoods in three cities, because access to print resources is important, because this access "has both an immediate and long-term effect on their vocabulary, background knowledge, and comprehension skills" (p. 127). They concluded that children's books were not readily available for purchase in these neighborhoods, labeling these neighborhoods as book deserts. Other scholarship has explored the availability of culturally relevant children's books. The concept of windows and mirrors is helpful for understanding why having diverse and inclusive children's books is important for all children (Bishop, 1982). Mabbott (2017) provides a nice explanation:

> The use of children's books as a way of reflecting (mirrors) a child's own experience is vital in order for that child to understand that she/he has value and worth in our society. To show a child another person's experiences (windows) that are quite different from her/his own transforms the child's view of that person into empathy. (pp. 511–512)

Hughes-Hassell et al. (2009) use critical race theory to explore diversity and inclusivity in transitional books, which are sometimes referred to as first or early chapter books, concluding that "white privilege is apparent in the publication of transitional books" (p. 11). The overwhelming majority of the transitional books that they analyzed had white characters, and it would be difficult for BIPOC students to find books that represent their identities. Furthermore, whenever a book did feature a more diverse set of characters, White characters were always present. Finally, most of the books were written by White authors, including all of the biographies about people of color. The authors of the study believe this sends a strong message that normalizes Whiteness.

In addition to the empirical literature related to literacy development, several articles related to culturally relevant, evidence-based school library practices have emerged.[2] Kumasi (2012) used Tupac Shakur's poem "The Rose That Grew from the Concrete" to introduce critical race theory and how it applies to the practice of school librarians. Hughes-Hassell (2013) shared best practices for serving Black and African American students based on the summit addressing African American male youth literacy. In the five essential elements, Hughes-Hassell highlights the importance of having school administrators and librarians who "evaluate research-based programs and services aimed at meeting the needs of African American youth" (Hughes-Hassell, 2013, p. 12). In addition, the publication *Knowledge Quest*, from AASL, dedicated a 2017 issue to connecting issues of race to the practice of school librarians. This issue included articles that address shifting the lenses by which librarians view students of color (Kumasi & Hughes-Hassell, 2017), collaborating with students to develop professional development for teachers about being culturally responsive (Bunner, 2017), creating annotated resource lists related to cultural competence (Cooke & Hill, 2017), and more.

CONCLUSION

Although racial segregation in public schools in the United States is now illegal, public schools are still highly segregated. Parents with the means to do so make decisions about where to live based on the quality of schools associated with particular cities or neighborhoods. However, not all parents have the means to make decisions about where to live, and these parents are disproportionately BIPOC. Because public school funding is intimately tied to local property taxes, this creates a separate and unequal educational experience for students, in which majority White school districts are well resourced and majority BIPOC schools are underresourced. Even in schools that are integrated, sorting and tracking practices disproportionately disadvantage BIPOC students and create further residential segregation in schools. This is compounded by the heavy-handed discipline and policing to which BIPOC students, particularly Black and African American students, are subjected. Black and African American history is not well integrated into many school curricula, often focusing on enslavement and the fight for Civil Rights, rather than highlighting the many contributions that Black Americans and African Americans have made throughout our nation's history. Although many Black and African American students do thrive in our public K–12 schools, the culmination of these practices, which have deep legacies in centuries of educational exclusion that denied Black Americans and African Americans the right to an education, results in persistent institutional equity and opportunity gaps for Black and African American children and youth.

Just as Dr. Lacy Jones indicated in her 1945 dissertation, racial issues within schools are also racial issues within school libraries. While there has not been a lot of research that explores Black and African American students' experiences with school libraries, we do have some evidence to support Dr. Lacy Jones's statement. The heavy-handed discipline and policing of Black and African American students is evident in Brown's (2007) research. In addition, some of the students in Brown's study perceived that the librarians had low expectations of them, perhaps even believing that they are or have the propensity to be violent. Just as broader educational research has demonstrated the importance of funding and resources to beginning to close institutional equity and opportunity gaps, the same is true for school libraries. School library impact studies have found positive outcomes for BIPOC students when full-time librarians are available and present in their schools (Coker, 2015; Lance & Kachel, 2018). Despite this, Pribesh et al. (2011) found that students enrolled in schools with higher concentrations of poverty were the least likely to have access to librarians and adequate library resources. Finally, some studies have found students perceive a lack of cultural representation within their library collections (Agosto & Hughes-Hassell, 2005), despite positive implications for racial identity development (Kumasi, 2008). Diversity and inclusion in reading materials for children and youth is a significant issue (Hughes-Hassell et al., 2009; Mabbott, 2017), meaning that intentionality in selecting culturally relevant materials is critical.

RECOMMENDED READING

AASL American Association of School Librarians. (2021). Black librarianship: Navigating race and creating change [Special issue]. *Knowledge Quest*, 49(4).

Brown, T. M. (2007). Culture, gender and subjectivities: Computer and internet restrictions in a high school library. *Journal of Access Services*, 4(3/4), 1–26.

Clotfelter, C. (2004). *After Brown: The rise and retreat of school desegregation*. Princeton University Press.

Ford, D. Y. (2013). Gifted underrepresentation and prejudice: Learning from Allport and Merton. *Gifted Child Today*, 36(1), 62–67.

Grant, G. (2011). *Hope and despair in the American city: Why there are no bad schools in Raleigh*. Harvard University Press.

Hughes-Hassell, S. (2013). Designing effective library services for African American youth. *School Library Monthly*, 29(6), 11–13.

Noguera, P. A. (2008). *The trouble with black boys . . . and other reflections on race, equity, and the future of public education*. Jossey Bass.

Orfield, G., & Lee, C. (2004). *Brown at 50: King's dream or Plessy's nightmare?* The Civil Rights Project, Harvard University. https://civilrightsproject. ucla.edu/research/k-12-education/integration -and-diversity/brown-at-50-king2019s-dream-or -plessy2019s-nightmare/orfield-brown-50-2004 .pdf

Pollock, M. (Ed.) (2008). *Everyday antiracism: Getting real about race in school*. The New Press.

Wiegand, W. A. (2021). Race and school librarianship in the Jim Crow South, 1954–1970: The untold story of Carrie Coleman Robinson as a case study. *Library Quarterly*, 91(3), 254–268.

NOTES

1. Housing policies have a significant impact on the racial diversity and funding of public schools. A detailed discussion is out of scope for this book, but Grant (2011) provides an overview of some of these practices.

2. This paragraph is certainly not exhaustive; we aim to provide a few examples of this kind of scholarship.

5

ACADEMIC LIBRARIES

OVERVIEW

In this chapter, we focus specifically on academic libraries and higher education. We begin by reviewing the historical exclusion of Black Americans and African Americans from institutions of higher education in the United States, as well as the development of historically Black colleges and universities (HBCUs) as sources of educational empowerment. While enrollment of Black and African American students in all postsecondary institutions has increased over the past four decades, degree completion rates remain low. We discuss institutional factors that contribute to these persistent equity gaps, including campus racial climate and culture. Finally, we provide an overview of the relevant LIS literature, including research that explores Black and African American students' library usage and their perceptions of library services and programs.

THE BROADER HIGHER EDUCATION CONTEXT IN THE UNITED STATES

Despite rich and ancient African intellectual traditions, higher education in the United States has a racialized history, much like that of public libraries and public education, which featured the exclusion of Black and African American citizens for more than a century. Indeed, Duster (2009) characterizes the first two-thirds of the history of higher education in the United States, until roughly the 1960s, as having "a decidedly apartheid-like character" (p. 99). Higher education in the United States began with private institutions that had two priorities—to train White men for (1) the clergy or (2) other kinds of professions, like law (Duster, 2009). It was not until the passing of the first and second Morrill Acts,[1] in 1857 and 1890, respectively, that institutions of higher education in the United States began to open their doors to a broader audience. Before the Morrill Acts, many colleges were mostly private institutions. However, this legislation provided states with land and funding[2] to create public-serving institutions, resulting in contemporary land-grant institutions (Duster, 2009). Higher education became a public good, both for the education that institutions provided and for their contributions to basic and applied research. In particular, the second Morrill Act addressed racial discrimination in higher education, requiring public institutions to be available to citizens of all races, though it permitted the creation of segregated public institutions.

Although the numbers were small, Black and African American students enrolled in and completed college degrees as early as the first half of the nineteenth century. This is remarkable and extraordinary considering that some states had laws that explicitly forbade teaching Black Americans and African Americans how to read, particularly those who were enslaved, and people caught educating Black Americans and African Americans faced criminal punishment (Duster, 2009). John Chavis is believed to be the first African American to enroll in a college; he attended what is now known as Washington and Lee University in 1799 (JBHE, n.d.). Alexander Lucius Twilight is believed to be the first African American to graduate with a college degree, which he earned at Middlebury College in 1823. He was followed by Edward Jones from Amherst College in 1826, John Brown Russwurm from Bowdoin College also in 1826, and Edward Mitchell from Dartmouth in 1828. Oberlin College was established in 1833, and it took a progressive stance toward enrollment, admitting both African Americans and women. Indeed, the first known African American woman to earn a college degree, Mary Jane Patterson, graduated from Oberlin in 1862. Despite these remarkable milestones, Wilder (2013) reminds us of the racialized origins of colleges and universities, including in the North, and their dependence on the enslavement of Africans and African Americans for survival.

Many HBCUs, both public and private, were established in the nineteenth century as well. Although segregation was more prominent in the South, HBCUs appeared across the country because racial discrimination against Black and African American citizens was widespread and prevalent. The first HBCU, the Institute for Colored People, now Cheyney University, was established in Pennsylvania in 1837. Haynes (2006) notes that the establishment of HBCUs really gained momentum after the Civil War and Emancipation, with 39 HBCUs being established between 1865 and 1890, which doubled the number of Black and African American citizens earning collegiate degrees. Many of these universities were supported by religious denominations that felt a duty to educate and inspire Black students for higher learning, including

the Presbyterian Church, which founded Lincoln University in Pennsylvania, and the Methodist Episcopal Church, which founded Wilberforce University in Ohio (Haynes, 2006). As mentioned previously, one factor that explains this dramatic increase was that so many Black Americans and African Americans, both enslaved and free, had been denied the right to an education, including basic literacy skills. Because of this, many of these newly formed institutions focused on providing their students with a secondary education and preparing them to succeed in higher education. However, teaching Black and African American citizens even the most basic of literacy skills was a contentious subject with many White citizens, particularly in the South.

Because of this, tensions about the role and mission of HBCUs arose between two prominent African American leaders, Booker T. Washington and W. E. B. DuBois (Haynes, 2006). Based on his experience at his alma mater, Harvard University, DuBois supported a liberal arts education, similar to the kind of education that many White students were receiving in predominantly White institutions. On the other hand, Washington, who had been born into enslavement and was a graduate of an HBCU, believed that teaching African Americans agricultural skills and vocational training would set them up for the most success. Duster (2009) argues that Washington took more of an accommodationist approach to mitigate White rage and "publicly avoid any appearance of direct competition for higher educational access with Whites" (p. 103). Although Washington initially advocated for vocational training, he eventually changed his viewpoint and worked with "White philanthropists and established Tuskegee College as a place where Blacks could get training to become doctors and lawyers" (Duster 2009, p. 104). These two men had very different educational experiences due to the geography of their upbringing—one in the North and one in the South—on which they likely based their advocacy for the type of higher education that would enable success for Black Americans and African Americans in both the short and long terms, success that necessarily depended on White citizens being comfortable with the possibility of Black Americans and African

Americans becoming more equal in terms of educational attainment and economic status. By 1943, almost 400 Black Americans and African Americans had attained their PhDs, almost 100 of which were in the sciences (Sammons, 1990). As a result, the contributions of Black and African American scholars and professionals were becoming more visible through scholarly and news media publications.

Until roughly 1970, the overwhelming majority of Black and African American college students attended HBCUs. Black students were being excluded from many predominantly White institutions (PWIs), and HBCUs provided a kinder and more supportive atmosphere for their Black students and actively groomed them for leadership roles within society. Duster (2009) writes that "only two percent of all African Americans attending U.S. higher education institutions were enrolled in traditionally White colleges and universities" in 1967 (p. 100). However, by the mid-1970s enrollment patterns had shifted, and "the majority of Black college students were enrolled in traditionally White institutions" (Duster, 2009, p. 100). Black and African American citizens contributed to the higher education enrollment boom that occurred after World War II and throughout the second half of the twentieth century. A variety of contributing factors included the Servicemen's Readjustment Act of 1944 (i.e., the G.I. Bill), increased access to federal financial aid, and desegregation of traditionally White institutions (Harvey et al., 2004).

Indeed, the college enrollment rates of Black and African American students and their overall representation within postsecondary institutions has increased over the past several decades. In 1976 just under 10 percent of all enrollments in postsecondary institutions in the United States were Black or African American students. Their representation has increased to just over 13 percent in 2018, which is lower than the peak of 15 percent in 2010 (NCES, 2019d). Furthermore, the percentage of Black and African American young adults (i.e., adults between the ages of 18 and 24) enrolling in higher education increased from 31 percent in 2000 to 36 percent in 2018, with a peak of 38 percent in 2016 (NCES, 2019b). This slightly narrowed the enrollment opportunity gap between White young

adults and Black and African American young adults from 8 percent in 2000 to 6 percent in 2018. In fall 2018 HBCUs enrolled about 9 percent of all Black and African American students enrolled in postsecondary education (National Center for Education Statistics, 2019d, 2019e).

A factor that drove the increase in college enrollment among Black and African American students, especially at PWIs, was affirmative action (Beasley, 2011). Although many of the high-profile affirmative action lawsuits have been related to admission to postsecondary education, affirmative action has its roots in employment and hiring practices for federal contractors and its primary beneficiary has been White women (Tatum, 2017). The roots of affirmative action can be traced back to World War II, when A. Philip Randolph threatened a march of 100,000 Black Americans and African Americans on Washington, DC, to protest racially discriminatory employment practices (Duster, 2009). As a result, "President Franklin Roosevelt agreed to create a federal Fair Employment Practices Commission" to address this issue, though it was largely ineffective (Duster, 2009, p. 105). This paved the way for the more contemporary form of affirmative action that affects employment more generally and postsecondary admissions more specifically.

Colleges and universities, particularly more selective institutions, voluntarily implemented race-based admissions decision making given their overwhelmingly White student bodies. This has not come without controversy and frequent lawsuits in which the Supreme Court has gotten involved based on the decades-old (and incorrect) argument that "racial preferences have placed underqualified blacks at prestigious institutions while displacing their more deserving white counterparts" (Beasley, 2011, p. 3). These arguments do not raise the hypocrisy of the admission practices concerning legacy applicants (i.e., students who have a parent or parents who graduated from the institution) and how those disproportionately benefit wealthy White students (Howell & Turner, 2004). Indeed, one study (Arcidiacono et al., 2016) "found that [at Harvard University] 43 percent of white students admitted to Harvard University were recruited athletes, legacy students, children of faculty and staff, or on the dean's interest list—applicants whose parents or relatives have donated to Harvard" (Silva, 2019). This was true for less than 16 percent of Black and African American students who were admitted. Given the historical exclusion of Black and African American students at PWIs, the category in which most selective institutions fall, this is not surprising. A more extreme example of this kind of power and privilege recently received national media attention. Fifty people, including celebrities, business executives, and athletic coaches, were charged for using bribes to gain their children admission to elite institutions (Friedman, 2019). The strategies used include "cheating on college entrance exams" and in classes and "bribing coaches and administrators to designate applicants as recruited athletes (when they were not athletes) to gain admission" (Friedman, 2019, "Allegations" section, para. 1). The man who organized this scheme—William "Rick" Singer—said "he helped children of over 750 families fake their way into a college or university of their choice" (Lambe, 2021, "What Is" section, para. 3).

Other key elements missing from the critiques of affirmative action are that we narrow definitions and measures of merit and that there are objective and accurate ways to measure and assess merit (Moses, 1999). One common assessment is performance on the SAT or ACT, which many selective institutions no longer require because of evidence that they unfairly disadvantage students of color. Part of this is likely due to the institutional equity and opportunity gaps in K–12 public education discussed in the previous chapter. Not only are White students more likely to attend well-resourced schools with credentialed and experienced teachers and college preparatory classes, including AP or dual enrollment classes, but they are also more likely to be able to access test preparation services due to racialized socioeconomic disparities. Not surprisingly, students in higher-income families make use of test preparation services more than students in lower-income families (Buchmann et al., 2010). Moses (1999) highlights that both merit and capacity for success are important to consider, and those cannot be measured by test scores alone. She

writes, "'Merit' is a cultural construct that has historically benefited certain elite people. Merit has always been multidimensional, but it has become more and more unidimensional as it is used to keep the club elite" (Moses, 1999, p. 273). The lawsuit of Abigail Fisher, a White applicant to the University of Texas at Austin, highlights the problematic nature of these kinds of assessments. Fisher believes that she was racially discriminated against because she was rejected and 47 applicants whom she perceived to have lower qualifications (e.g., grade point average and standardized test score) than her were admitted. However, only 5 of the 47 applicants were students of color, and "168 black and Latino students with grades as good as or better than Fisher's were also denied entry into the university that year" (Darling-Hammond & Dintersmith, 2017, "First Piece" section, para. 5).

Despite positive trends in terms of enrollment and overall representation, trends related to degree completion and graduation continue to pose a concern. Black and African American students who enroll in four-year institutions have one of the lowest degree completion rates based on the most recent data from NCES. In 2010 the six-year degree completion rate for Black and African American students enrolled in four-year institutions was 40 percent, which is significantly lower than for the two highest groups—Asian/Asian American students at 74 percent and White students at 64 percent (NCES, 2019c). However, Black students have better degree completion rates when they attend HBCUs. Although the raw numbers indicate that HBCU degree completion rates might be lower than those of other institutions (Gordon et al., 2020), researchers have found that when compared with non-HBCU institutions with similar characteristics (e.g., size, finances, quality of instruction, etc.), as well as controlling for student-level characteristics, the graduation rates at HBCUs are roughly 10 percent higher than at their non-HBCU peer institutions (Franke & DeAngelo, 2018; Gordon et al., 2020). Despite representing less than 3 percent of colleges and universities in the United States, HBCUs graduate 70 percent of Black physicians and dentists and 50 percent of Black engineers (Williams & Ashley, 2004). In addition, HBCUs "produce the greatest number of minority teachers" (Fenwick, 2001, p. 22). Tuskegee University graduates 80 percent of Black veterinarians, and Florida A&M University has surpassed Harvard University in National Achievement Scholars among Black students. Black students who attend an HBCU tend to have higher grade point averages and higher acceptance rates into graduate or professional schools than their peers who attend a PWI (Williams & Ashley, 2004). Akua (2015) states that HBCUs have a history of accepting Black students into their institutions when other higher learning institutions had no interest in or willingness to accept them within their doors, which likely results in a supportive environment for Black students.

Factors that contribute to lower overall degree completion rates for Black and African American students, particularly at PWIs, include poor campus racial climate and campus racial culture. Museus et al. (2012) draw upon Bauer (1998) to define campus climate as the "'*current* perceptions, attitudes, and expectations that define the institution and its members,' and it is often used to understand how people *feel* within a particular environment" (p. 29). Several studies have investigated perceptions of campus racial climate, how these perceptions differ based on race, and how these perceptions shape academic outcomes (Cabrera et al., 1999; George Mwangi et al., 2018; Rankin & Reason, 2005; Solórzano et al., 2000). Rankin and Reason (2005) found that students of color are more likely than White students to perceive the campus racial climate to be "racist," "hostile," and "disrespectful," as well as finding classroom settings to be "less welcoming" (p. 52). Many studies have found that students of color, including Black and African American students, experience harassment and microaggressions on their college campuses (George Mwangi et al., 2018; Rankin & Reason, 2005; Solórzano et al., 2000). Rankin and Reason share, "Fully one third of students of color in our sample reported having experienced harassment, compared to 22% of White students" (Rankin & Reason, 2005, p. 57). For White students, the harassment was often related to gender (i.e., women). The students who participated in Solórzano et al.'s (2000) study, all of whom were Black or African American, identified some of the common microaggressions they face, including low expectations from instructors, feelings of invisibility, the omission of their experiences or history within classes, feeling tokenized, not being picked for study groups, and assumptions about being there due to affirmative action. These experiences led to students feeling isolated and exhausted. The Black and African American students in George Mwangi et al.'s (2018) study indicated that these experiences led them to feel like they needed to be positive representatives of their race. Sometimes this was related to feelings of empowerment and pride, but other times it was related to feelings of pressure and obligation. Regardless of the motivation, students indicated that this meant they often needed to be on top of their game nearly all the time. This was also a phenomenon that we saw among the students in our study, particularly when discussing the role of family in reading and using the public library.

Campus racial culture is more stable but also more difficult to capture in some ways, and Museus et al. (2012) indicate that this culture is often neglected when exploring issues related to campus racial climate. Part of this is because campus racial culture is so deeply embedded in the history and operations of the institution. Kuh and Hall (1993) indicate that campus culture includes

> institutional history, mission, physical settings, norms, traditions, values, practices, beliefs, and assumptions that guide the behavior of individuals and groups in an institution of higher education which provide a frame of reference for interpreting the meanings of events and actions on and off campus. (p. 2)

Campus racial culture then interrogates how this culture can "differentially shape the experiences of various racial and ethnic groups and can function to oppress racial minority populations within a particular institution" (Museus et al., 2012, p. 32). Some elements of campus racial culture are a bit easier to identify than others. For example, many of us have probably recognized that numerous buildings on our campuses are named after White males or that portraits memorializing past leadership are primarily of White males. Depending on our institutions, we might fail to acknowledge or be completely unaware of how the institutions participated in and/or benefited from the transatlantic trafficking of enslaved Africans (Wilder, 2013). Many of us, particularly White readers, might forget or be unaware that many of our institutions, including libraries, excluded Black and African American citizens from enrollment until relatively recently, either intentionally or implicitly.

A visible legacy of this exclusion is the lack of representation of people of color among our faculties, which also likely affects the campus racial climate for students of color. According to recent NCES data, 75 percent of full-time faculty in postsecondary institutions were White. Black males and Black females accounted for only 3 percent each (NCE, 2020). While the representation was slightly higher for Black males and females at the assistant professor level—5 percent each—the percentage dropped to 2 percent each at the professor level. While institutions have witnessed a significant increase in the diversity of students who are enrolling, an increase in the number of faculty of color has not been keeping pace. A recent Pew Research Center study found that overall the number of faculty of color has increased by 10 percent between 1997 and 2017, but the number of Black and African American faculty has increased only 1 percent during that same time period (Weissman, 2019). A different study from the TIAA Institute has found that most of the gains in representation for faculty of color have been in adjunct or contingent faculty roles and not tenure track positions (Finkelstein et al., 2016). This study uses the umbrella category underrepresented minority (URM), which does not include nonresident aliens or Asian American faculty. While there were significant gains in URM faculty in full-time tenured (60.9 percent) and tenure track (30.1 percent) positions between 1993 and 2013, the increase in full-time non–tenure track faculty was double and quadruple those rates at 142.9 percent. In addition, the percent change for URM part-time faculty during the same period was 229.8 percent.

Although faculty of color are not responsible for resolving issues related to negative campus racial climate, their lack of representation among full-time, tenure track faculty likely means that fewer advocates for positive changes to campus racial climate are in leadership positions. In addition, many faculty of color might feel marginalized and isolated in the same ways the students of color report given their small numbers and the prevalence of stereotypes, microaggressions, and other forms of discrimination. The lack of faculty of color and a negative campus racial climate are likely mutually reinforcing. Negative campus racial climate likely affects the number of Black and African American students who decide to pursue a career in the academy and the number of faculty of color who are ultimately retained. In addition, this means Black and African American students who do aspire to a career in higher education have limited role models. Furthermore, negative campus racial climate likely influences the retention and persistence of Black and African American college students, which affects the potential pipeline of faculty of color into the professoriate.

A positive aspect of the collegiate curriculum is that all students likely have increased access to courses or curricula about race and ethnic studies. Indeed, many general education curricula require students to take at least one course that relates to diversity, though students can usually choose from among courses that address aspects of diversity other than race. These courses can be powerful in terms of Black and African American students' racial-ethnic-cultural (REC) identity formation (Tatum, 2017). Indeed, helping Black and African American students tap into positive aspects of their cultural heritage can transform how they view themselves (Akua, 2012; Tatum, 2017). Tatum (2017) shares her own experience as a college student. Despite enrolling in a PWI, college was the first time that she had the opportunity to really explore her identity through her academic coursework. This coursework, in addition to the cohort of Black and African American friends that she made, helped her to take pride in her identity as a Black woman in a way that had not been possible for her in high school. Curricula, as well as cocurricular and extracurricular activities, that allow Black students to explore their identities promote "group esteem," which Tatum describes as "feeling good about one's group" (Tatum, 2017, p. 166). Tatum highlights the importance of safe and supportive spaces for Black and African American students to discuss their experiences with one another, as well as with faculty and staff of color, particularly at PWIs, as this can also contribute to positive REC development and feelings of group esteem. Indeed, others have found that Black and African American students have developed counterspaces, in which they can collectively cope with negative aspects of campus racial climate (Beasley, 2011; Solórzano et al., 2000).

Finally, we would like to take a moment to discuss recent issues related to campus racial climate, particularly after the election of now former President Trump in 2016. While there have been overt forms of racial discrimination on college campuses for centuries, the past few years have seen a resurgence in these overt acts, including the dissemination of White nationalist or White supremacist literature, vandalism that involves racial slurs, and mock lynchings. Although not all hate crimes are racially motivated, it is worth noting that reported hate crimes on college campuses have been increasing since 2015, with a 25 percent increase from 2015 to 2016 (Bauman, 2018). In 2018, hate crimes based on race accounted for 43 percent of the hate crimes on college campuses based on data analyzed by NCES (2021a). The combination of microaggressions, campus hate crimes, and racial issues on a national scale have resulted in student activism on college campuses (George Mwangi et al., 2018; Tatum, 2017). Student activists have been holding "protests, sit-ins, walkouts, and die-ins" (George Mwangi et al., 2018, p. 466), some of which have occurred in library spaces, as well as issuing lists of demands to college administrators (Tatum, 2017), including taking down White statues that exemplify past racial biases (Stewart, 2020). Although some of these have resulted in concrete changes, such as the resignation of President Tim Wolfe and Chancellor R. Bowen Loftin from the University of Missouri, students reported being met with scorn and vitriol from other White students. George Mwangi et al. (2018) provide examples of the kinds of responses that many of these student activists faced from their peers. On the other hand, several students were heartened by the participation of White students, faculty, and administrators in these activities.

ACADEMIC LIBRARIES LITERATURE

Compared to public and school libraries, there has been more research about how Black and African American students use and perceive academic libraries. This may be due, in part, to Mallinckrodt and Sedlacek's (1987) finding that studying in an academic library had a statistically significant relationship with the retention of Black and African American students. Whitmire (1999, 2003, 2004, 2006) was a leader in this research, stating that earlier research about library usage and experiences had not adequately accounted for race and ethnicity. For three of her studies, Whitmire (1999, 2003, 2004) analyzed data collected through national-level student experience and satisfaction surveys with large sample sizes. In these studies, she found that, in general, "African American students used the library resources more frequently than the White students did" with the exception of "checked citations in things read" and "found materials by browsing in stacks" (Whitmire, 1999, p. 35) and that "writing experiences, faculty experiences, the number of non-assigned books read, course learning activities, and class year were associated with more frequent academic library use" for African American students (Whitmire, 2003, p. 158). In her 2006 study, Whitmire used observational data and answers to locally developed questionnaires to explore how Black and African American students used and experienced the library as a place. She found that Black and African American students were "well-represented in the library" (Whitmire, 2006, p. 64) and reported using the library at least once a week. They chose to use the library as place because they could be productive in an environment where they knew other people, though socialization was the least important reason they came to the library. Shoge (2003) also explored the library usage of Black and African American students. The undergraduate students in her study used the library because they perceived it had positive implications for their academic performance. The students used the library for electronic resources and print materials, as well as to study, do homework, and do research. They, however, did not rank getting help from a librarian as a motivating factor for using the library.

Previous research also examined Black and African American students' usage of and experiences with specific kinds of reference services. Shachaf and Snyder (2007) conducted a content analysis of 94 virtual reference interactions of White and African American distance education students at a single institution. They found that African American students, in general, had more messages per interaction and were more likely to ask follow-up questions in their interactions. African American students were also more likely to ask topical known-item questions, whereas White students were more likely to ask technical questions. Hudson (2010) explored the preferences of students with various racial and ethnic backgrounds related to the provision of mobile reference services. Her motivation to conduct this research was due to data reporting the prevalence of people of color using wireless, mobile devices to access the internet. In her study, students of all racial and ethnic backgrounds indicated similar usage of social media networks and smartphones. However, African American females and White males expressed the highest likelihood that they would make use of mobile reference services staffed by a live librarian. Cox, Gruber, and Neuhaus (2019) reported the racial/ethnic demographics of the participants in their study about research consultations; however, they did not use this information in their analysis of the data.

Other research has examined instructional partnerships that target and support students of color. In many cases, these partnerships were developed with offices that support diversity and inclusion, and the library embedded an instructional component into an existing program. Several of these partnerships focused on formal programs that have been established at the national level, often with federal funding, to support the academic success of students of color and to encourage them to pursue graduate studies, including Upward Bound, the McNair Scholars Program, the Summer Research Opportunities Program (SROP), and the Educational Opportunities Program (Clarke, 2012; Love, 2009; Simmons-Welburn &

Welburn, 2001). However, Holmes and Lichtenstein (1998) describe a partnership that was developed with a locally developed program called the African Americans Partnering Talent Summer Academy. The focus of libraries' contributions to these instructional partnerships varies, with some covering research skills (Holmes & Lichtenstein, 1998; Love, 2009; Simmons-Welburn & Welburn, 2001) and others providing an introduction to using the library and its resources (Clarke, 2012; Love, 2009; Simmons-Welburn & Welburn, 2001). Simmons-Welburn and Welburn (2001) describe how their approach to content evolved as their partnership with Upward Bound matured, noting the focus of their sessions

> shifted from teaching library use to providing grounds for building individual knowledge on locating information in support of class assignments and other academic activities, independently analyzing results and refining search strategies, and seeking out sources to aid in using chosen information. (p. 13)

A related facet of this literature focuses on supporting Black and African American students during instruction sessions or through research assignments. Mortimore and Wall (2009), librarians at an HBCU, reviewed literature related to motivational theories, including academic self-concept, and relevant research about Black and African American students to think about how this could inform and shape their instructional work. Based on their extensive research, the authors offer four practical recommendations for other librarians: (1) "faculty and librarians must provide a unified voice of authority and encouragement to students," (2) "instructional librarians must be effective teachers," (3) "librarians and faculty must work together to develop curricula and assignments that motivate African-American college students and that permit librarians to engage students in the information search process," and (4) "student encouragement and support cannot be perceived as limited to or ending with one instruction session" (Mortimer & Wall, 2009, pp. 38–39). Folk's (2018) research focusing on first-generation students' experiences with research assignments supports these recommendations. She found that when students of color—all of whom were Black or African American—had the opportunity to engage their identities, lived experiences, or career aspirations in their research assignments, it seemed to result in a learning orientation to the assignment, which appeared to have positive implications for the demonstration and development of their information literacy.

Around the same time that Mortimore and Wall (2009) published their recommendations, critical librarianship was gaining momentum within academic librarianship, particularly as it relates to information literacy (Elmborg, 2006), library instruction (e.g., Accardi, 2013; Accardi et al., 2010), and pedagogy (e.g., Pagowsky & McElroy, 2016a, 2016b). A critical lens to instructional work considers the ways in which students' identities shape their experiences, both with information use and with their overall educational journey, demanding us to consider the ways in which oppressive power structures, including those that promote or maintain White supremacy, shape those experiences. Furthermore, critical approaches to this instructional work require us to think about how to empower students in the face of those oppressive power structures, as well as how we dismantle those structures. Pashia (2016) provides an example of how one might incorporate critical information literacy and critical pedagogies into a course intending to develop students' information literacy by explicitly having them explore and reflect upon how White supremacy pervades their campus and the information they find and use. Despite the emergent popularity of critical librarianship, the document that shapes much of our teaching and learning efforts, *Framework for Information Literacy for Higher Education* (ACRL, 2015), does not explicitly address the role of race (Folk, 2019; Rapchak, 2019).

Some scholarship has explored the racial climate of academic libraries for communities of color from a variety of perspectives. Warner (2001) discusses how Whiteness is reinforced both by historical and current academic library practices, including the selection of materials, cataloging, and the provision of library services. Brook et al. (2015) examine the manifestation and reinforcement of Whiteness in academic libraries

by conducting a critical discourse analysis on several of the profession's guiding documents and highlight the racialized aspects of academic library spaces, library staffing, and the provision of reference services. Elteto et al. (2008) explored the library experiences of both students of color and White students at a diverse, urban university and found that "students of color who responded use the library more than do their White counterparts; but, paradoxically, they still felt that the library was slightly less welcoming of them" (p. 334), including the White library staff. Numerous studies of the experiences of librarians of color within academic libraries (e.g., Alabi, 2015a, 2015b; Curry, 1994; Preston, 1998) demonstrate an unsupportive work environment for our colleagues of color. Some factors contributing to a poor racial climate for librarians, including Black and African American librarians, include microaggressions, low expectations of competence, and reduced opportunities for advancement.

There have been numerous publications throughout the past three decades about how academic libraries have attempted to meet the needs of students of color, including the creation of inclusive spaces. Love (2009) categorizes the evolution of some of these initiatives, noting that early publications focused primarily on services for and by students of color, such as the development and implementation of the peer information counselor programs at the University of Michigan (MacAdam & Nichols, 1989) and the University of Arizona (Norlin, 2001). These programs hired and trained students of color to provide reference support. The hope was that having a diverse student staff at the reference desk would not only benefit the student employees hired as information counselors but also create a more welcoming environment for other students of color. The next phase of these initiatives included outreach to various campus multicultural centers to determine the library needs of students of color (e.g., Harrell & Menon, 2002; Norlin & Morris, 1999; Walter, 2005). Another common tactic is creating book displays and exhibits that reflect the diverse identities included on campus (e.g., Maloney, 2012). More recently, many academic libraries have hosted the Race Card Project (https://theracecard

project.com) to normalize the discussion of race and how it impacts users' lived experiences, not just in the library, but throughout their lives. When libraries have hosted the Race Card Project, it has provided their communities with the opportunity to share anonymously their thoughts about, questions about, or experiences with race, while also elevating (through displays) the voices of the community on this topic.

Recent research has focused more on the perceptions and experiences that Black and African American students hold about and have with libraries and librarians rather than focusing solely on the ways in which they use the library. Katopol (2012) interviewed Black and African American graduate students enrolled at PWIs to examine the students' "perceived effect of race on information activities" (p. 6). The students perceived that the library did not have works by Black scholars, and White students had increased access to information related to their research interests. Furthermore, they did not believe that librarians would have the expertise to support their topics when they were racially related, and they turned more often to peers for support rather than their professors or librarians. Stewart et al. (2019) surveyed Black and African American students enrolled at PWIs to explore their perceptions of academic library spaces, focusing on four different dimensions: employee interactions, library as place, information need, and perceived welcomeness. Students perceived the library to be welcoming, and both library as place and information need were significantly correlated with that perception, meaning that they were more or less satisfied with their ability both to use the library space and to access relevant information sources. Interactions with library employees was not statistically significant, which might be related to Shoge's (2003) earlier finding that getting help from a librarian was not an important reason for using the library for this student population.

The most in-depth study to date was recently conducted by Duke University Libraries (Chapman et al., 2020), and it explores Black and African American students' perceptions of inclusiveness when using the libraries. The research team used a variety of data collection methods, including information interviews, focus groups, Photovoice sessions, and library satisfaction survey results, to learn more about both undergraduate and graduate students' experiences. The research team integrates findings related to libraries into a broader discussion about the students' experiences at the university, and they are explicit in recognizing the historical racialized exclusionary practices of the university. Although Black students reported feeling safer in library spaces than on campus in general, they did not strongly agree with the statements about safety in library spaces at the rate that their White peers did. Space was important to feelings of welcomeness in libraries. The students discussed the prevalence of portraits of White males in many library spaces and the lack of a space dedicated to Black culture and history. Students also indicated that several spaces needed to be modernized in terms of décor and suggested more vibrant colors be used in those spaces. Furthermore, many students spoke about how fraternities dominated certain library spaces, including study rooms, which made them feel uncomfortable. In general, students spoke highly of library services, and textbook lending was especially important to the undergraduate students. However, the research team uncovered an interesting tension between our professional best practices for the provision of reference services and students' perceptions of their help-seeking experiences. Whereas many librarians and library staff approach reference interactions as learning opportunities—teaching students how to use the website or search the catalog—this was often perceived as condescending or patronizing and suggested to students that they were bothering the staff with their questions.

CONCLUSION

Similar to K–12 public education, higher education has made progress in enrolling and graduating Black and African American students over the past several decades. However, persistent opportunity and equity gaps remain, and Black and African American students continue to have lower rates of enrollment and degree completion. This is due in part to campus racial cultures that have been historically based on serving wealthy, White students, and their contemporary legacies continue to create barriers to the development of inclusivity and a true sense of belonging. In addition, experiences with discrimination and microaggressions, as well as a notable lack of Black and African American faculty, create a hostile campus racial climate for many Black and African American students attending PWIs. Although Black and African American students have more positive outcomes at HBCUs, enrollment trends shifted in the 1970s, and today more Black and African American students are attending PWIs than HBCUs. Depending on the institution, Black and African American students typically have more opportunities to take courses and engage with curricula that affirm their identities when they reach higher education, as well as creating peer groups who help them cope with the stress of being a college student and the discrimination they face if attending a PWI. Despite these supports, many Black and African American students face additional stress at PWIs compared to their White peers due to unwelcoming or hostile racial climates.

In term of LIS scholarship, Black and African American students seem to be better represented in the academic libraries literature relative to other library types, though their voices are still mostly absent. This is likely due, in part, to increased expectations of many academic libraries to conduct research, present at conferences, and/or publish in journals, though this certainly is not an expectation of all academic librarians. Furthermore, a non-LIS study about undergraduate student retention in the 1980s found that studying in an academic library had a statistically significant relationship with the retention of Black and African American students (Mallinckrodt & Sedlacek, 1987), which may have prompted further inquiry within academic libraries. Library usage studies, based primarily on quantitative data, indicate that Black and African American students use their academic libraries, though some of their activities might differ from those of their White peers (Shoge, 2003; Whitmire, 1999, 2003, 2004, 2006). Scholarship also reveals that many libraries have partnered with diversity and inclusion programs with the intention of supporting BIPOC students. However, only two studies elevate the voices of

Black and African American students (Chapman et al., 2020; Katopol, 2012). This research confirms that the Black and African American students who participated do use their academic libraries (Chapman et al., 2020). However, these students did not perceive that the library had materials that would meet their information needs or that the librarians would be able to support their research, while they did indicate that spaces represented Whiteness and that reference interactions could be perceived as condescending (Chapman et al., 2020; Katopol, 2012). This last finding is particularly relevant given the underrepresentation of Black and African American librarians in academic libraries and parallels issues in universities more generally. Maybe Black and African American students feel more comfortable seeking help from faculty and staff who look like them, and this can have two significant results. First, BIPOC students might not reach out for support that is available to them. Second, BIPOC librarians might be expected to serve all of the BIPOC students, as well as addressing organizational needs in terms of equity, diversity, and inclusion. While racial representation is just one piece of a complex puzzle, it is a significant one. Given the overwhelmingly White nature of the academic library profession, it is troubling that so many programs and services are being built to serve various student populations without an understanding of their expectations, needs, and experiences in libraries.

RECOMMENDED READING
Chapman, J., Daly, E., Forte, A., King, I., Yang, B. W., & Zabala, P. (2020). *Understanding the experiences and needs of Black students at Duke*. https://dukespace.lib.duke.edu/dspace/handle/10161/20753

Curry, D. A. (1994). Your worries ain't like mine: African American librarians and the pervasiveness of racism, prejudice and discrimination in academe. *The Reference Librarian*, 21(45–46), 299–311.

George Mwangi, C. A., Thelamour, B., Ezeofor, I., & Carpenter, A. (2018). "Black elephant in the room": Black students contextualizing campus racial climate within US racial climate. *Journal of College Student Development*, 59(4), 456–474.

Haynes, B. (2006). *Black undergraduates in higher education: A historical perspective.* Metropolitan Universities, 17(2), 8–21.

JBHE *The Journal of Blacks in Higher Education.* (n.d.). *Key events in Black higher education: JBHE chronology of major landmarks in the progress of African Americans in higher education.* https://www.jbhe.com/chronology/

Mortimore, J. M., & Wall, A. (2009). Motivating African-American students through information literacy instruction: Exploring the link between encouragement and academic self-concept. *Reference Librarian*, 50(1), 29–42.

Moses, Y. T. (1999). Race, higher education, and American society. *Journal of Anthropological Research*, 55(2), 265–277.

Rapchak, M. (2019). That which cannot be named: The absence of race in the Framework for Information Literacy for Higher Education. *Journal of Radical Librarianship*, 5, 173–196.

Strand, K. J. (2019). *Disrupting Whiteness in libraries and librarianship: A reading list (Bibliographies in Gender and Women's Studies).* University of Wisconsin. https://www.library.wisc.edu/gwslibrarian/bibliographies/disrupting-whiteness-in-libraries/

Thurgood Marshall College Fund. (n.d.). *History of HBCUs.* https://www.tmcf.org/history-of-hbcus/

NOTES

1. The Morrill Acts established land-grant institutions, thus acknowledging higher education, both in terms of teaching and research, as a public good. The land and money used to establish land-grant institutions were frequently generated from the theft of indigenous land.

2. While the creation of public institutions was generally a positive development, many of the land-grant universities were established on lands that were acquired through the federal government's theft of land from Native American tribes. Furthermore, funding often came from the sale of lands that had been stolen from Native Americans. As Nash (2019) wrote, "And they would not exist as land-grant institutions except for the forced removal of American Indians from their lands."

6

FRAMEWORKS FOR EXPLORING RACE AND LIBRARIES

If you have read the three preceding chapters, we hope you will agree with our statement that libraries in the United States and the institutions with which they are associated indeed have racialized histories, histories that have excluded and disenfranchised Black and African American communities. The legacy of this racialization, exclusion, and disenfranchisement has implications for how Black and African American users experience our libraries today. Based on our conversations with students who participated in our study, which are reported in *Narratives of (Dis)Engagement: Exploring Black and African American Students' Experiences in Libraries*, we argue that remnants of these racialized histories are still evident in their experiences with contemporary libraries. In this chapter, we provide overviews of two theoretical frameworks—critical race theory and theories of Whiteness—that can be used to explore and unpack Black and African American users' experiences with libraries and consider the ways in which White librarians and library staff contribute to these racialized experiences. Both of these theoretical frameworks enable the exploration of race in library experiences and the ways in which BIPOC library users may experience discrimination, marginalization, or discomfort. However, they approach that exploration from different lenses. An exploration of the racialized experiences is critical to fulfilling librarianship's professed interest in equity and social justice because "the presence and effects of systemic racism are often hidden in race-neutral approaches to service delivery that fail to account for the differential experience of racialized and marginalized groups" (Matthews, 2020). In other words, to create equitable and just experiences, spaces, collections, programs, and services, we must critically examine the ways in which race affects contemporary library experiences. In *Narratives of (Dis)Engagement*, we apply these theories to the racialized library experiences that students in our study shared with us.

CRITICAL RACE THEORY

Library practitioners and scholars have used critical race theory (CRT) throughout the past decade to explore various facets of libraries and librarianship, including library collections (Bowers et al., 2017), library leadership development programs (Hines, 2019), instruction and pedagogy (Leung & López-McKnight, 2020), professional standards and guidelines (Brook et al., 2015; Rapchak, 2019), LIS research (Stauffer, 2020) and discourses (Kumasi, 2013), information theory (Dunbar, 2008), and the LIS curriculum (Gibson et al., 2018). The application of CRT to LIS and librarianship provides an opportunity to refute the myth that libraries are race-neutral spaces. Given that librarianship is an overwhelmingly White profession, race might not seem salient for the majority of librarians and library staff. However, for people who are racialized in American society (i.e., everyone who is not perceived or considered to be White), race is present as they navigate their daily lives, including their experiences within libraries. To equitably support and serve our BIPOC communities and create antiracist library environments, we must explore the role of race in their lives and their library experiences.

CRT has gained a lot of national media attention recently, as many politicians are actively seeking to ban CRT from K–12 public education. Some of these politicians and their supporters believe that CRT "teaches students to disparage the U.S. and works to sow racial divisions in classrooms" (Manchester, 2021). These beliefs are rooted in a color-evasive ideology that promotes the idea that even acknowledging race inherently creates tension or conflict (Bonilla-Silva, 2018; Burke, 2019). Some believe that CRT promotes reverse racism, although based on the definition of racism that we provided in the introduction, we believe that reverse racism does not actually exist.[1] Proponents of CRT argue that it provides a foundation to identify the ways in which racism is built into our institutions, exploit opportunities to challenge the status quo, and rebuild key institutions on equitable, just, and antiracist principles and values. In other words, the avoidance of discussions about race and the racialized history of the country perpetuate (systemic) racism because it obscures the ways in which racism manifests in contemporary society. Because of the current national controversy, it is important to discuss what CRT is and what CRT is not.

CRT has its roots in critical legal studies in the latter half of the twentieth century and was shaped by prominent legal scholars, such as Kimberlé Crenshaw and Derrick Bell. At that time, critical legal studies examined the ways in which laws and the criminal justice system oppressed and marginalized people of color. As CRT developed, it became interdisciplinary in nature and began to be influenced by and applied to other fields of study and professions (Yosso, 2005). Although CRT focuses on the role of race in the

oppression of people of color, it also takes into account other aspects of identity, such as gender, ability, and socioeconomic status. While there is general agreement about the key elements or core tenets of CRT, scholars have framed and articulated these elements in various ways. Matthews (2020) shares the five core tenets of CRT in education that were outlined by Ladson-Billings and Tate (1995):

- Race and racism are defining characteristics of society as opposed to isolated acts or events of discrimination.
- Ideologies of objectivity, meritocracy, neutrality, and colour-blindness often shield dominant groups from identifying their privilege in ways that sustain power.
- Analyses must be interdisciplinary and historical to disentangle dominant ideologies.
- It is a transformative social justice framework to eliminate all forms of oppression.
- It centres and is guided by the experiential knowledge of those whose lives are impacted by every day and systemic experiences of oppression and injustice. (as quoted in Matthews, 2020, p. 4)

Yosso (2005) highlights the same elements in her work about community cultural wealth, though, for her, CRT is not just interdisciplinary but transdisciplinary. Bowers et al. (2017) draw upon Dunbar (2008) to highlight five key elements of CRT—interest convergence, microaggressions, counternarratives, intersectionality, and social justice (p. 162). In the next several paragraphs, we discuss various elements of CRT using literature reviewed in previous chapters of this special report, as well as introducing additional literature when appropriate.

Central to CRT is a recognition that racism is an everyday and lived reality for people of color in the United States. Yosso (2005) explains that "CRT starts from the premise that race and racism are central, endemic, permanent and a fundamental part of defining and explaining how US society functions" (p. 73). Racism can range from negative interactions with people who are explicitly or implicitly prejudiced against people of color to attempting to navigate obstacles and barriers presented by systemic racism.

One of the many reasons why it is important to highlight this reality is that many White people take for granted the ways in which race shapes the everyday experiences of people of color, thus remaining completely invisible to them because this is not something that White people experience firsthand. The invisibility of racism, including systemic racism, based on Whiteness is discussed in more depth later in this chapter. In previous chapters, we reviewed literature that highlighted the ways in which organizations, including banks, governmental bodies, and schools, have historically discriminated and currently discriminate against Black and African American citizens. Historically, this includes practices like redlining and Supreme Court decisions related to racial desegregation of public schools. Currently, this includes the overrepresentation of Black and African American students in special education programs and their underrepresentation in gifted student programs.

This core tenet is evident in the LIS literature, even in scholarship that was not explicitly drawing upon CRT. In terms of public libraries, race defined who could use a particular library until relatively recently. Race also shapes perceptions of the cultural relevancy of collections (Agosto & Hughes-Hassell, 2005) and whether or not an inquirer who is perceived to be Black or African American receives a response (Giulietti et al., 2019). Race shapes where people live, what schools they go to, and how those schools are resourced, among a myriad of other school-related outcomes. Pribesh et al. (2011) found that the type of school a student attends based on the concentration of poverty affects the quality of their school library. This is significant as school library impact studies have found that having a high-quality library is correlated to positive educational outcomes (Coker, 2015; Lance & Kachel, 2018). Scholarship related to academic libraries has indicated that race shapes perceptions about collections and the ability of librarians to help Black and African American students with their research (Katopol, 2012), as well as the experience of condescension when seeking help at a service point (Chapman et al., 2020).

A related element of CRT is the regularity with which people of color experience racial microaggressions. Originally coined by Pierce (1970), the term microaggression refers to the "brief and commonplace daily verbal, behavioral or environmental indignities, whether intentional or unintentional, that communicate hostile, derogatory, or negative attitudes toward stigmatized or culturally marginalized groups."[2] Dunbar (2008) describes how microaggressions tend to be "subtle" or "non-verbal" (p. 44). Examples of microaggressions include backhanded compliments, such as a White person complimenting a person of color for being so articulate, or subtle behaviors, such as a White woman noticeably clutching her purse more tightly when walking past a Black male. Taken individually, microaggressions might seem more like an annoyance and less serious than more explicitly racist acts, such as the use of a racial slur or the presence of systemic racism. However, BIPOC tend to experience microaggressions with regularity, and the accumulation of these recurring and frequent experiences is what makes them so insidious. Oluo (2019) writes, "The cumulative effect of these constant reminders that you are 'less than' does real psychological damage. Regular exposure to microaggressions causes a person of color to feel isolated and invalidated" (p. 169). Because of the regularity of microaggressions, BIPOC tend to expect to experience racism through both subtle or outright uncivil acts of bias. While BIPOC are legally protected from employment discrimination, this kind of protection does not typically prevent subtle forms of everyday racism like microaggressions, nor are perpetrators typically held to account for these acts.

Curry (1994) provides examples of microaggressions that Black and African American academic librarians face from their White peers. One of these examples is the assumption that a Black or African American librarian was hired due to affirmative action, and that they are somehow less qualified for the position. These kinds of assumptions have serious implications for Black and African American librarians' performance, success, and overall career trajectories within the profession. Alabi (2015a) explored the experience of microaggressions among academic librarians and found that librarians of color experienced microaggressions on the job, which was not the case for White librarians. In a companion study, Alabi (2015b) analyzed reported microaggressions of academic librarians of color and created nuanced categories, including microassaults, microinsults, microinvalidations, and environmental microaggressions. These experiences led to librarians of color feeling isolated and had implications for recruitment and retention of librarians of color.

CRT also includes the interrogations of practices that are purportedly objective, neutral, and based on merit. These practices are often shaped by Whiteness because White people historically and currently tend to be in decision-making, leadership, or powerful positions. In terms of educational spaces, this can manifest in decisions related to discipline and punishment, tracking and sorting, and admissions in colleges and universities. Hathcock (2015) and Galvan (2015) provide examples of how this manifests in recruitment and hiring decisions within libraries and how these practices reproduce an overwhelmingly White profession. Kumasi (2013) frames this tenet as "Whiteness as property," meaning that "whiteness has been framed as both the preferred and normal state of being" (p. 108). She applies this tenet to young adult library services with a focus on literacy and information literacy, which have been dominated by and normalized as a cognitive approach, rather than considering the ways in which libraries could incorporate "home and community literacy perspectives" (Kumasi, 2013, p. 109).

Counternarratives or counterstories are another core tenet of CRT. Counternarratives often present a different perspective on the dominant narratives primarily constructed by White people. An example of a counternarrative from the previous chapters is Ray's (2015) study about African American students and school discipline in the Los Angeles area from the students' perspectives. The dominant narrative in this example would be that of the teacher and their justification for punishing a student for a particular behavior. However, when the students were asked to provide their perspectives, they often shared that the teacher made assumptions based on their behavior and acted on those assumptions rather than speaking to the students to determine what was happening. As discussed earlier, Brown's (2007) study exploring the school library experiences, with a focus on computer usage, of a diverse group of students at a large, urban high school provides a similar example. Remember Malik, the student who was kicked off the computer while researching a car website for a school project before he had a chance to explain that he was using it for academic purposes. He believed that the White library media specialists thought he was a "bad kid" (Brown, 2007, p. 16), and that perception likely led the librarian to make assumptions about Malik's motives rather than engaging him in a conversation that could have supported his academic needs. Kumasi (2013) frames this tenet as "voice" and highlights the emphasis that CRT places on honoring the lived experiences of people of color: "CRT scholars recognize the centrality of the experiential knowledge of people of color and view this knowledge as legitimate, appropriate, and critical to understanding, analyzing, and teaching about racial subordination" (Kumasi, 2013, p. 105).

The final core tenet that we address here is that of interest convergence, which was originally defined by Bell (1980). Interest convergence argues that the "the interest of blacks in achieving racial equality will be accommodated only when it converges with the interests of whites" (Bell, 1980, p. 523, as cited in Dunbar, 2008, p. 12). In his 1980 publication, Bell argued that the Civil Rights Act of 1964 was passed, not out of beneficence to Black Americans and African Americans, but as a response to the international reputation damage that Jim Crow was causing to the United States (Kumasi, 2013). McGhee's (2021) recent book provides many examples of how racist practices across our society, including in education, employment, and health care, actually harm everyone, though people of color are disproportionately harmed, and how surfacing these harms can be the first step in addressing systemic racism. McGhee calls the result of this interest convergence the *solidarity dividend*. Kumasi (2013) applies interest convergence to the LIS context, noting that White librarians experience benefits when they implement diversity programming. She poses several questions that librarians can ask to uncover interest convergence in their own practices, including these:

> Do I capitalize on youth initiatives that promote diversity and equality while subconsciously holding a cultural deficit perspective about youth of color themselves? Do I view youth of color as unfortunate victims in a fundamentally just society? Do I transfer the stereotypical images that play out in the media about youth of color onto those whom I might encounter in my library? (Kumasi, 2013, pp. 107–108)

In terms of the last question, the students in our study shared that they perceived librarians as having made assumptions about them and their behavior based on racial stereotypes. One of the authors, Tracey, has had similar conversations with Black and African American teen users, noting that they likely would have been kicked out of a library for talking or laughing if the librarian would not have been Black.

Through our discussion of CRT, we hope that it is clear that CRT is a framework for centering the voices and lived experiences of BIPOC with the goals of understanding how race shapes their everyday lives and identifying the ways in which racism oppresses and marginalizes BIPOC. In other words, CRT is meant as a tool to empower BIPOC and move toward the creation of a just, equitable, and antiracist society. It is not a tool that is meant to oppress White people or create racial division, though discomfort, shame, guilt, and anger might be common albeit unproductive responses that White people have when systemic racism is presented to them. Some White people might see this as the creation of racial division or conflict where there previously was none. However, that is a myopic perspective in that racial division has always existed; it simply was not previously evident to White people because it has not affected them. This kind of reaction is not inherent to the application of CRT; rather it is symptomatic of a color-evasive society.

WHITENESS

Another theoretical frame that is increasingly being used in LIS scholarship is Whiteness. Different theories of Whiteness have been used to explore the nature of libraries and librarianship (Brook et al., 2015; Espinal, 2001; Galvan, 2015; Pawley, 2006; Schlesselman-Tarango, 2016; Warner, 2001), reference services (Hathcock & Sendaula, 2017), archival work (Ramirez, 2015), library spaces (Beilin, 2017), and research methodologies (Stauffer, 2020). Whereas CRT centers the voices and lived experiences of BIPOC, theories related to Whiteness provide a framework for analyzing and identifying how White cultural values and White supremacy shape much of our daily lives, including institutions such as schools and libraries. Theories of Whiteness can help to identify how we might change our institutions to become more inclusive and equitable based on the experiences that are elevated and centered through critical race theory.

Galvan (2015) provides useful definitions of Whiteness and discusses how it manifests in our behaviors, often unbeknownst to White people. She writes, "Whiteness is 'ideology based on beliefs, values behaviors, habits and attitudes, which result in the unequal distribution of power and privilege.' . . . Beliefs, values behaviors, habits and attitudes become gestures, enactments, and unconsciously repetitive acts which reinforce hegemony" (Galvan, 2015, Defining Whiteness section, para. 2). Often both the abstract and behavioral elements of Whiteness remain invisible to many White people because White people typically do not go through the same racial identity development that people of color do and therefore do not think of themselves in racialized terms (Tatum, 2017). In other words, they often do not reflect upon their own race and how it manifests through daily activities or systemically through social institutions, like schools and libraries. Also, through centuries of White-dominated discourse, Whiteness has become the unquestioned status quo in society in the United States.

Feagin (2020) provides a comprehensive overview and discussion of how Whiteness has become the dominant ideology in the United States through the concept of the white racial frame. Although the white racial frame predates the colonization of the territory that we now call the United States, Feagin highlights the centrality of the subordination and dehumanization of Indigenous Americans, Black Americans, and African Americans through land theft and enslavement to the beginnings of the United States. Both of these cruel practices were central to the economic prosperity of the White colonizers, and therefore, it was critical to perpetuate the superiority of White Americans, particularly men, as a justification for the ways in which they were treating Indigenous Americans and African Americans. Although enslavement ended in the late 1800s, other practices, such as Jim Crow laws and redlining, were used to continue the subordination of Black and African American citizens. Even today, as we arguably are attempting to move toward a more inclusive and just society, the racial hierarchy that has White people at the top and Black and African American citizens at the bottom is maintained by individuals' beliefs and prejudices as well as institutions and systems that were designed to privilege White citizens. Feagin argues that many view the institutionalization of this racial hierarchy as the "routine organizational operation of society," which is how systemic racism remains unchallenged and persists to the present day (Feagin, 2020, p. 168).

Okun (2021) presents several characteristics of the ways in which Whiteness and White supremacy manifest, many of which are particularly relevant to professional environments. Characteristics include the belief that there is one right way to do this (which includes paternalism, perfectionism, objectivity, and qualified), the either/or binary, denial and defensiveness, right to comfort and fear of conflict, individualism, quantity over quality, worship of the written word, and a sense of urgency. Some of these might seem familiar already, as they were included in discussions of the characteristics of a color-evasive culture/society and are aligned with the core tenets of CRT.

One framework to explore and analyze the manifestation of Whiteness in institutions, such as schools and libraries, is the concept of White institutional presence (WIP; Gusa, 2010), which was first introduced in the LIS literature by Brook et al. (2015). Gusa (2010) defines WIP as the "customary ideologies and

practices rooted in the institution's design and the organization of its environment and activities" (p. 467). In other words, WIP allows for an examination of the taken-for-granted practices, systems, and values that largely go unexamined because Whiteness often remains invisible to White people and is often treated as the status quo or the normal modus operandi. Gusa offers four characteristics of WIP:

- White ascendancy—This includes elements of superiority and entitlement based on "Whiteness's historical position of power and domination" (Gusa, 2020, p. 472).
- Monoculturalism—This asserts that cultural values, including the creation of knowledge, related to Whiteness are correct and objective. In other words, there is only one acceptable appropriate way of thinking or acting.
- White blindness (i.e., race invisibility)[3]—This makes discussions about race inappropriate and preserves White people's emotional comfort, as well as their White privilege.
- White estrangement—This is the "distancing of Whites physically and socially from people of color," thus making cross-racial interactions difficult, tense, and uncomfortable (Gusa, 2020, p. 478).

In the discussion that follows, we also draw upon other literature to provide examples of how these frames manifest in contemporary libraries. Many of the examples that we share do not fit neatly into a single frame, and elements of multiple frames are often evident in a single example. We do not address race invisibility specifically, as that has been highlighted throughout this special report.

The entitlement that accompanies White ascendancy includes "a sense of ownership White people may assume over a space" (Gusa, 2020, p. 472). Kumasi (2013) provides an example of this, noting how one of the participants in her study said, "The library is like her [the librarian's] house" (p. 104). In the study conducted by Chapman et al. (2020), Black and African American students spoke about how the architecture and decor of library spaces also indicated the pervasive Whiteness of the library and of campus. Both Beilin (2017) and Brook et al. (2015) discuss how the architecture and decor of library spaces can also reinforce monoculturalism, in that it could serve to canonize greater thinkers or scholars, most of whom tend to be White men. Another aspect of White ascendency is the presence of security and/or police in libraries. As Robinson (2019) points out, security presence in library spaces can reinforce for people of color that they are not welcome or that they are being watched, even though White library staff and users may believe that this presence is not problematic and ensures the safety of all.

Monoculturalism is also evident in LIS scholarship. For example, the Black graduate students who participated in Katopol's (2012) study indicated that they did not believe that White librarians would be able to help them with topics related to their identities, and that the libraries might not have the materials needed to support that research. Brown (2007) found that White librarians in a diverse, urban high school had very stringent notions about what kinds of information are acceptable for the students' academic work, and she discusses how these beliefs were not culturally inclusive, quite the contrary, in fact. Agosto and Hughes-Hassell (2005) also found that Black teens who participated in their study believed that their public library did not have culturally relevant materials. Chapman et al. (2020) highlight the misalignment between Black students and library staff when they ask for helping finding material. While it is common practice in many libraries to use these kinds of interactions to educate users about how to use the library and its resources, this was viewed as condescending and perceived as signaling to the user that they should know how to do this already. Monoculturalism also aligns with one of the characteristics that Okun (2021) identified—the belief that there is one right way to do something.

White estrangement is also evident in other LIS studies, such as Agosto and Hughes-Hassell (2005), in that the African American students who worked in the library did not seem to make meaningful connections with the librarians and library staff. In other cases, White estrangement seems to overlap with other elements of WIP. Disregard or unawareness of the culture and history of Black and African American communities, as well as other communities of color, seem to result in White ascendancy and entitlement (Brown, 2007; Robinson, 2019), as well as race invisibility and monoculturalism (Beilin, 2017; Brook et al., 2015; Chapman et al., 2020; Katopol, 2012).

CONCLUSION

Because librarianship is an overwhelmingly White profession, many librarians and library staff are likely unaware of the various ways that race affects the daily lives of our library users of color. Other scholars have highlighted the problematic assumption that libraries are race-neutral spaces due to our mission to support and serve our communities, many of which have diverse demographics (Honma, 2005; Gibson et al., 2017). The implicit and explicit biases of library employees do not simply disappear the moment they enter the library, and it is unreasonable to assume that biases that exist in other facets of library employees' lives do not manifest when they are working or interacting with Black and African American community members. Likewise, Black and African American community members bring their experiences with White people with them into library spaces, and there is no reason to expect that they believe that their experiences with libraries are somehow going to be different from those in other places that they regularly visit, such as schools, doctors' offices, or grocery stores.

We presented two frameworks to explore these experiences and provide some insight into factors that contribute to them. CRT and theories of Whiteness, such as WIP, are good complements, especially for a profession that is overwhelmingly White and has resisted, for the most part, explorations of Black and African American library users' experiences. CRT provides some insight into the experiences of people of color, experiences that White people typically do not have. It reminds us to center the lived experiences and voices of people of color. When we do this and truly listen, we are gifted opportunities to improve our services, spaces, collections, and programming to support our communities. In this way, we can take steps to become equitable, just, and antiracist organizations.

Theories of Whiteness, including WIP, illuminate the ways in which Whiteness manifests and can be toxic. The manifestation of Whiteness is likely invisible to many librarians and library staff who are White because White cultural values are taken for granted, particularly those embedded in organizational culture, and are considered to be the status quo or the normal way of operating. However, this status quo can be injurious to our Black and African American community members, as well as to other communities of color, in that their identities can be marginalized by our behaviors, our spaces, and our services. In other words, it maintains White supremacy and toxicity. Even if this maintenance is unintentional, the result for our communities of color is still harmful. WIP, in particular, provides four elements that can be used to analyze and interrogate our organizational culture, including our library operations and our spaces, to identify areas for change and improvement.

RECOMMENDED READING

Brook, F., Ellenwood, D., & Lazzaro, A. E. (2015). In pursuit of antiracist social justice: Denaturalizing whiteness in the academic library. *Library Trends*, 64(2), 246–284.

Feagin, J. R. (2020). *The white racial frame: Centuries of framing and counter-framing* (3rd ed.). Routledge.

Gusa, D. L. (2010). White institutional presence: The impact of whiteness on campus culture. *Harvard Educational Review*, 80(4), 464–489.

Kumasi, K. (2013). "The library is like her house": Reimagining youth of color in LIS discourses. In A. Bernier (Ed.), *Transforming young adult services: A reader for our age* (pp. 103–113). ALA Neal-Schuman. Retrieved from Digital Commons@ Wayne State. http://digitalcommons.wayne.edu/slisfrp/95

Matthews, A. (2020). Racialized youth in the public library: Systemic racism through a critical theory lens. *Theory and Research*, 15(1), 1–17.

Okun, T. (2021). *White supremacy culture characteristics.* White Supremacy Culture. https://www.white supremacyculture.info/characteristics.html

Schlesselman-Tarango, G. (2016). The legacy of Lady Bountiful: White women in the library. *Library Trends*, 64(4), 667–686.

NOTES

1. White people might face racial prejudice from individual BIPOC; however, BIPOC have not historically had, nor do they currently have, the same collective power to build or rebuild institutions that discriminate against, oppress, or marginalize White people.

2. Microaggression. (2021, March 26) In Wikipedia. https://en.wikipedia.org/wiki/Microaggression

3. We recognize the problematic nature of using the term blindness here, as it is ableist. We will refer to this characteristic as race invisibility throughout the rest of the book.

7

CONCLUSION

In this report, we reviewed literature related to the historical exclusion and disenfranchisement of Black Americans and African Americans by libraries and the institutions with which they are associated, such as K–12 public schools and institutions of higher education. Given that Black Americans and African Americans were only given access to these institutions within the past 50 years or so, it stands to reason that the legacy of this exclusion likely manifests today. For example, we have discussed the prevalence of residential segregation and how that affects the K–12 experiences of many Black and African American children. We have discussed persistent racial opportunity and equity gaps that Black and African American children experience in K–12 and higher education due to the historical denial of a quality education. However, we found a disturbing gap in LIS literature that explores the experiences of Black and African American library users or evaluations of programs that are intended to engage this user population. This is particularly notable given the profession's espoused commitment to inclusivity and equity at many levels, including ALA and its divisions and among our individual libraries.

Although several studies have examined Black and African American students' library usage, particularly in academic libraries, most of these used closed-ended surveys (Elteto et al., 2008; Shoge, 2003; Stewart et al., 2019; Whitmire, 1999, 2003, 2004). This survey research has provided an important foundation for understanding the ways in which Black and African American students use libraries, but the findings do not provide much insight into how Black and African American students experience libraries. Survey research does not provide the researcher with the opportunity to probe participants' experiences, perceptions, and feelings more deeply with follow-up questions, nor does it typically provide participants the opportunity to provide detailed elaboration of their responses to questions.

Going beyond usage to explore experiences of BIPOC library users is critical given both the history of racialized exclusion in libraries and the institutions with which we are associated and the overwhelmingly White nature of all sectors of the profession. Many White librarians and library staff have a genuine and sincere desire to serve equally all users who visit their libraries, both physically and virtually. However, as a profession, we do not often discuss how our libraries and institutions were not necessarily built to serve BIPOC users, nor do we collectively consider how the legacy of centuries of racial exclusion and outright discrimination (e.g., enslavement and Jim Crow) in libraries and schools, as well as across our society more broadly, manifests in our services, programs, policies, practices, resources, collections, and spaces today. Furthermore, because White librarians and library staff do not experience racism firsthand, nor do they typically go through a process of racial identity formation (Tatum, 2017), the manifestations of Whiteness and White supremacy in our libraries and educational institutions frequently remain unnoticed and invisible to many White librarians and library staff. Compounding this issue is that color-evasive racism has become the new racism, and many White people believe that noticing or discussing race at any level makes them a racist (Bonilla-Silva, 2018; Burke, 2019).

At this point, some readers might be thinking that we are suggesting that White librarians and library staff are not able to adequately support our Black and African American library users. While this interpretation is understandable, this is not what we believe. To prepare White librarians and libraries to adequately serve Black and African American library users moving forward, we believe that we need more research, evaluation, and assessment about how Black and African American library users experience the library. Furthermore, we would like to acknowledge that many individual libraries, librarians, and library school faculty are working hard to make change within their own libraries, programs, and communities. Several examples within public libraries are available through a report published by GARE (Sonnie, 2018). However, it is difficult to find information that evaluates and assesses the effectiveness of these programs, analysis that would highlight effective practices that actually engage Black and African American library users and benefit the entire profession.

We also enthusiastically believe that our profession desperately needs to recruit and retain more BIPOC librarians. However, a deep discussion of this point is outside the scope of this report, and there is a wealth of literature on this topic despite the fact that we have not been able to achieve this goal (e.g., Alabi, 2018; Brook et al., 2015; Cunningham et al., 2019; Espinal et al., 2018; Galvan, 2015; Hathcock, 2015; Kendrick & Damasco, 2019). However, we believe that the focus of this chapter—equity-minded, race-centered systematic inquiry—may also have a positive effect on the

recruitment and retention of BIPOC librarians, as our goal is to help librarians contribute to inclusive, equitable, and antiracist organizational cultures.

Matthews (2020) recently wrote, "Libraries are a racial space where the dominance of whiteness is sustained through unacknowledged norms, values, and structures that have operationalized white ways of being and knowing as invisible and normative in both our profession and our institutions" (p. 5). To move beyond the race evasiveness of the profession, we focus on a call to action in the remainder of this report:

> Encouraging libraries to undertake equity-minded, race-centered assessment, evaluation, and research that provide evidence of the needs, expectations, and experiences of our diverse user communities and disseminating this work broadly.

Again, there are a number of actions that librarians, library staff, and library organizations can take to promote racial equity, including an equity-minded overhaul of recruitment, hiring, retention, and promotion practices; organizational learning (e.g., cultural competency workshops); and culturally inclusive and relevant programming. We do not want to understate the importance of these, but we believe that these topics have been the focus of many discussions in the profession. What has received less attention is cultivating an equity-minded approach to data collection, analysis, and use as a method for the profession, specifically White librarians, to move away from a race-evasive approach to their practice.

EQUITY-MINDED, RACE-CENTERED SYSTEMATIC INQUIRY (I.E., ASSESSMENT, EVALUATION, AND RESEARCH)

As a profession, we really do not have a good understanding of how the racialized and exclusionary histories of our institutions contemporarily manifest in the library experiences of BIPOC users, particularly Black and African American library users. As we have discussed in the previous chapters, there has been some research exploring Black and African American library users' experiences, particularly in academic libraries, but, in general, their voices, including their needs, expectations, and experiences, are absent from our scholarly literature. It is possible that individual libraries across all sectors of the profession are doing assessment and evaluation work that either focuses on this user population or disaggregates data by race. However, if this work is being done, it is not being widely disseminated. This would not be terribly surprising, as assessments and evaluations tend to be used internally for decision making and program/service improvement. However, when these kinds of assessments and evaluations remain internal, the entire profession does not benefit from them.

There are likely several reasons why our scholarly literature is lacking in this area, and all of them are linked to the color-/race-evasive nature of our society and the profession. We imagine that a significant factor is White librarians' discomfort with discussions about race and the resultant lack of motivation to engage this topic, leading to ignorance about the fact that race could affect users' experiences in libraries (and should be explored) or the (un)conscious desire to maintain the Whiteness of the profession and the expectation that BIPOC library users and colleagues should continue to conform to White cultural values or the status quo. In addition, it is certainly possible that this kind of systematic inquiry is deemed less important or less valuable by colleagues who are responsible for making employment decisions, such as managers or tenure and promotion committees. Our BIPOC colleagues might feel that their employment status or professional reputation could be threatened if they undertake this work, in that their colleagues, including managers, could view race-centered assessment or research as unpleasant, polarizing, or threatening. Even if conducting this kind of work does not result in negative consequences in terms of employment status, their peers and colleagues could form unwarranted opinions based on stereotypes—"She's so angry" or "It's always about race with them"—which could lead to an uncomfortable work environment and compound issues related to upward mobility within an organization. A recent, high-profile example of this is Nikole Hannah-Jones's initial denial of tenure from the University of North Carolina at Chapel Hill presumably for her leadership in the development of the *New York Times*'s 1619 Project, which "aims to reframe the country's history by placing the consequences of slavery and the contributions of Black Americans at the very center of the United States' national narrative" (https://www.nytimes.com/interactive/2019/08/14/magazine/1619-america-slavery.html).

Based on the lack of systematic inquiry about Black and African American library users, we believe that our profession is currently existing in a state of negligence based on Harper and Quaye's (2015) discussion of the importance of intentionality in serving and supporting BIPOC college students. They state that "simply providing services" is not enough to support BIPOC students (Harper & Quaye, 2015, p. 6), and the belief that it is enough is based on "magical thinking"—as if the benefits of the service provision "will accrue as if by magic" (Chang et al., 2005, pp. 10–11, as quoted in Harper & Quaye, 2015, p. 6). Part of this magical thinking includes the belief that basic interactions across races will lead to an understanding of diverse users' needs. Instead, professionals working with BIPOC populations need to develop intentionality, and "solutions must be grounded in students' actual experiences, reflective of their unique backgrounds and interests, and designed with both broad and specific implications in mind" (Harper & Quaye, 2015, p. 7). The remainder of this section discusses how we can move toward intentionality through systematic inquiry, or the collection, analysis, and use of data in research, assessment, and evaluation.

Before we delve more deeply into a discussion about what we think is important and how we can move forward, we would like to offer a word of caution and a caveat. Our BIPOC library users need library professionals who genuinely care about them; listen carefully to what they share in terms of needs, expectations, and experiences; and advocate for resources that support those needs equally compared to other user populations. Our BIPOC users do not need White saviors or heroes.[1] In addition, what follows is not intended to be a comprehensive guide to doing this work, though it would be helpful if someone would write that guide. The text that follows is meant to provide some overarching considerations for our profession as we strive to center and elevate the voices and experiences of BIPOC library users and minimize the presence of White privilege and supremacy in our profession.

As we discussed in the introductory chapter, racism is not just about individual actors who hold prejudiced beliefs. Racism is built into our institutions through policies and practices that (dis)empower communities based on socially constructed racial categories. Although there have been attempts to identify the ways in which racism and White privilege and supremacy manifest in libraries, as a profession, we do not have much systematically collected data or published researched to draw upon. GARE (https://racialequityalliance.org) has developed a toolkit that "proactively seeks to eliminate racial inequities and advance equity" and "integrate explicit consideration of racial equity in decisions, including policies, practices, programs, and budgets" (Nelson & Brooks, 2016, p. 4). GARE has partnered with public libraries across the country through their Libraries Interest Group to implement these ideals in their programming and initiatives (Sonnie, 2018). GARE's Racial Equity Toolkit identifies six elements that are intended to move

organizations through planning, implementation, and accountability (Nelson & Brooks, 2016). Two of these six elements highlight the importance of data in designing and evaluating racially equitable initiatives. In the planning stages, neglecting data, both quantitative and qualitative, could mean that initiatives are developed based on false assumptions and ultimately result in the reproduction of Whiteness in libraries. In addition, evaluation or assessment is crucial to determining the success of these initiatives in meeting their goals. In other words, effective racial equity work requires us to consult multiple sources of data when we are planning or updating our services and programs, as is the integration of assessment and evaluation practices into our plans. Hughes-Hassell (2013) echoes the importance of data for designing school library services for Black and African American children, directing this call to action at both school administrators and school librarians. She writes that school librarians should "engage in ongoing evaluation of resources, services, and programs; and use data both to develop responsive services and to advocate through equitable outcomes" (Hughes-Hassell, 2013, p. 12).

Focusing on equity gaps in higher education, McNair et al. (2020) also argue that the use of data is

BOX 7.1

Defining Assessment, Evaluation, and Research

In this section, we discuss systematic inquiry, which includes research, assessment, and evaluation, because different librarians will have different motivations for collecting, analyzing, and using data, all of which are valid and valuable to our libraries, the communities we serve, and the profession. For example, academic librarians who have faculty status will likely need to conduct research, whereas evaluation might be the priority of public librarians. School librarians and academic librarians might be interested in assessment of learning. We believe the strategies that we discuss are broadly applicable to each of these activities, so we do not offer an in-depth discussion about their similarities and differences. We briefly discuss each of these in this box to help contextualize the discussion in this section.

Research

Typically, research is intended to contribute to generalizable knowledge within the profession that can be used to inform theory building, future scholarship, or professional practice. The findings of research are often broadly applicable and not specific to a single organization.

Evaluation

"Evaluation is a form of inquiry that seeks to address critical questions concerning how well a program, process, product, system, or organization is working. It is typically under-taken for decision-making purposes and should lead to a use of findings by a variety of stakeholders" (Russ-Eft & Preskill, 2009, p. 6).

Assessment

"Assessment is the systematic collection, review, and use of information about educational programs undertaken for the purpose of improving student learning and development" (Palomba & Banta, 1999, p. 4).

critical in addressing institutional racial inequities, particularly when the data are disaggregated by racial
categories. However, it is not enough to simply collect, analyze, and use race-related data—these practices must be undertaken with an equity mindset to be
effective. They define *equity-mindedness* as

> the mode of thinking exhibited by practitioners who
> are willing to assess their own racialized assump-
> tions, to acknowledge their lack of knowledge
> in the history of race and racism, to take respon-
> sibility for the success of historically underserved
> and minority student groups, and critically assess
> racialization in their own practices as educators
> and/or administrators. (McNair et al., 2020, p. 20)

In other words, to be equity-minded is also to be
antiracist. When an equity-minded approach is taken
to program planning and assessment, the goal is to
address policies, processes, systems, or cultural values
that disadvantage certain user groups based on their
race and other demographic characteristics. This is in
stark contrast to a deficit frame, in which we attempt to
fix the users or their behavior, or a diversity frame, in
which we attempt to fix employees through workshops
and trainings (Bensimon, 2005). However, race- and
color-evasive ideologies that are ingrained in many
of us, particularly White colleagues, pose a potential
barrier to doing true equity-minded assessment
and evaluation. McNair et al. (2020) present several
potential obstacles, including claiming not to see
race, not being able or willing to notice racialized
consequences, skirting around race, substituting race
talk with poverty talk, the pervasiveness of White
privilege, and the incapacity to see institutional racism
in familiar routines (pp. 21–51). The authors provide
equity-minded responses to each of these obstacles
so readers can reflect on how to combat race- or
color-evasive responses when they arise in either a
colleague's response or their own.

Just as in diversifying our organizations and creating inclusive environments, our BIPOC colleagues
should not be solely responsible for undertaking race-
centered systematic inquiry. We all share the responsibility of understanding the needs and experiences of
our library users, regardless of our own racial and

ethnic backgrounds. Our BIPOC colleagues are disproportionately called upon to lead diversity and
inclusivity initiatives and mentor other BIPOC colleagues or students, which can lead to feelings of
tokenization and burnout. Furthermore, our BIPOC
colleagues may have experienced that their conclu-
sions, recommendations, or concerns are not made a
priority or think that they will be dismissed. However,
if our BIPOC colleagues are interested in taking the
lead or participating in this work, their perspectives,
experiences, and expertise should be honored at all
stages of the process, and they should be given the
resources needed to be successful, including time,
money, and organizational respect. Because the profession is overwhelmingly White, however, White
librarians and library staff must participate in these
practices to move from negligence to intentionality.
This can lead to some potential issues, however. For
many reasons, White librarians and library staff
should proceed with caution when conducting race-
centered systematic inquiry. Even when White people
have good intentions, they have not experienced a
racialized world and may make assumptions in the
design, data collection, analysis, and interpretation
stages that are unwarranted or counterproductive.

There are several ways to address this issue. The
first is to use professional networks and communities
to find out if there is a BIPOC colleague who would be
interested in collaborating on this work. Potential collaborators include, but are not limited to, another
librarian, a faculty member or teacher in a different
discipline, a graduate student (including LIS students), or a community leader. If you proceed down
this route, conversations about what collaboration
means, who will be responsible for what, and how to
maintain open and transparent lines of communication are essential. Even if the collaborators are peers,
the White colleague will likely hold more power than
the BIPOC colleague, and this should be acknowl-
edged and addressed. If the design calls for face-to-
face data collection, it is critical that BIPOC colleagues
are collaborators because many BIPOC library users
likely will not have the same level of trust with a
White interviewer as they would with another BIPOC
individual, and they might not feel comfortable or

safe discussing their needs or experiences in libraries, especially as they relate to race. Another option is working with a consultant, which could be a trusted colleague (e.g., librarian, teacher, faculty member, community leader) or a professional consultant. If working informally with a colleague, discussions about time, recognition, and compensation are also critical. Compensation could include an hourly rate or, depending on the nature of the relationship, treating your colleague to a meal or coffee during meetings about the project. Their time and labor should be honored. Finally, you could call upon members of existing advisory groups (e.g., board of trustees, Friends group, or student advisory group) or develop an advisory group for a specific project that is representative of the intended sample. If you are pursuing the latter, be clear about the nature of the work and the time commitment when recruiting members and once again consider how their time, energy, and expertise will be compensated. Finally, it is imperative that any White librarian or staff member embarking on this work be committed to continuous learning about race and racism as well as to reflection on their role in upholding Whiteness in the profession and the ways in which they benefit from Whiteness. We address this in our complementary special report, *Narratives of (Dis)Engagement: Exploring Black and African American Students Experiences in Libraries*.

There are helpful frameworks and methodologies available when pursuing race-centered, equity-minded systematic inquiry. As already mentioned a couple of times in this book, CRT is a guiding framework for centering race and its core tenets that can be useful when designing a race-centered study. Especially for White colleagues who are participating in this work, regularly reflecting on the tenets of CRT is one way to hold themselves accountable for ensuring that the experiences of BIPOC users are being centered and respected. Key questions based on CRT that might be used in the design phases as well as throughout the course of the study include the following:

- How are we acknowledging that BIPOC regularly experience racism as they navigate their daily lives? Have the White collaborators accepted this to be true?
- How are we centering, elevating, and honoring the voices and experiences of our BIPOC participants?
- Are we providing a safe space for our BIPOC participants to tell their stories?
- How are we accounting for the multiple aspects of our participants' identities, such as gender, religious affiliation, sexuality, or (dis)ability?
- How do we intend to use what we learn to transform our services, programs, policies, spaces, collections and resources, or organizational culture to be more just, equitable, and antiracist?
- How do we hold one another accountable for doing this work, and are we ready to make a commitment to having difficult conversations with one another?

While CRT centers and elevates the voices and experiences of BIPOC, theories of Whiteness can help to identity manifestations of Whiteness, including White supremacy and privilege, in our organizational culture, our service delivery, our programs, our policies, our collections and resources, and our spaces. Findings of equity-minded, race-centered research can help identify what needs to be dismantled and rebuilt in service of antiracism and equity and can serve as a useful complement to CRT. WIP (Gusa, 2010) is a useful starting point for interrogating Whiteness in libraries, as demonstrated by Brook et al. (2015) and in chapter 6 of this book. In addition, Bonilla-Silva (2018) has identified four frames that are central to color-evasive racial ideology[2]—which he and others have argued is the dominant form of racism in the United States today—abstract liberalism, naturalization, cultural racism, and minimization (see table 7.1). He also highlights some of the common semantic and rhetorical moves (i.e., coded language) that White people frequently use to explain away or dismiss racism. These frames can be helpful in interpreting data collected from White participants or can be used to frame a difficult conversation if a research

TABLE 7.1

The four frames of color-evasive racism as identified by Bonilla-Silva (2018)

Color-evasive frame	Description
Abstract liberalism	"Using ideas associated with political liberalism (e.g., 'equal opportunity,' the idea that force should not be used to achieve social policy) and economic liberalism (e.g., choice, individualism) in an abstract manner to explain away racial matters" (Bonilla-Silva, 2018, p. 56). Common examples include affirmative action or busing to address segregation.
Naturalization	"Explain[ing] away racial phenomena by suggesting that they are natural occurrences" (Bonilla-Silva, 2018, p. 56). Common examples include monoracial friendships/relationships and residential segregation.
Cultural racism	Using "culturally based arguments such as 'Mexicans do not put much emphasis on education' or 'blacks have too many babies' to explain the standing of minorities in society" (Bonilla-Silva, 2018, p. 56). Common examples include equity gaps in educational attainment, income, or generational wealth.
Minimization	Believing that "discrimination is no longer a central factor affecting minorities' life chances" (Bonilla-Silva, 2018, p. 57). Common examples include affirmative action or social policies to address racial equity gaps.

collaborator seems to be evading issues related to race and racism.

The methods that we use when undertaking systematic inquiry are also important, as they are representative of how we approach the nature of reality and knowledge construction, whether we are conscious of these beliefs or not. They also have implications for the methods we use to collect data and the nature of the interactions (or lack thereof) with participants. Mertens (2010) identifies four overarching paradigms, two of which are useful for guiding race-centered, equity-minded systematic inquiries—constructivist and transformative. In constructivism, reality and knowledge are socially constructed, and the constructivist paradigm rejects the notion that there is one objective reality that can be discovered or uncovered. Mertens explains that "knowledge is socially constructed by people active in the research process, and . . . researchers should attempt to understand the complex world of lived experience from the point of view of those who live it" (Mertens, 2010, p. 16). Consequently, constructivist studies often use qualitative

(e.g., interviews or focus groups) methods or mixed methods (i.e., a combination of both quantitative and qualitative methods) because they allow the researcher to probe a bit more deeply into a participant's experiences and tailor the conversation to that participant when there is some structure to the data collection method. In addition, constructivist studies often seek to assemble a sample that has diverse perspectives. For example, a researcher might limit a study's sample to Black or African American participants, but they might seek out participants with different gender identities or incomes or of varying ages.

The transformative paradigm is similar, but it goes one step further and centers the role that power plays in the participants' lived experiences (Mertens, 2010). Transformative studies are intentional in exploring "how and why inequities . . . are reflected in asymmetric power relationships" (Mertens, 2010, p. 21) and seeks to include "traditionally silenced voices . . . during the research process and the formation of the findings and recommendations" (Mertens, 2010, p. 33). Finally, transformative research explicitly seeks to use findings to enact social action or change, and "those who are most oppressed and least powerful should be at the center of the plans for action" (Mertens, 2010, p. 33). To avoid taking a paternalistic stance to "those who are most oppressed and least powerful" (Mertens, 2010, p. 33), researchers should intentionally integrate participants into all aspects of the research process, from designing to data collection to data analysis and interpretation to the dissemination of findings and recommendations. Like constructivist research, transformative research tends to employ either qualitative or mixed methods.

Participatory research is a method that is common to both the constructivist and transformative paradigms and is aligned with conducting race-centered, equity-minded systematic inquiry. Many colleagues automatically place participatory research within the transformative paradigm; however, Mertens (2007) notes that participatory methods are not inherently transformative and provides two different approaches to them (Mertens, 2010). The first is cooperative participatory research, which is aligned with the constructivist paradigm. In cooperative participatory research, the researcher(s), relevant stakeholders, and participants are coresearchers, insofar as "they identify a research problem and procedures that they want to work on together" (Mertens, 2010, p. 238). Although a diversity of representative perspectives, expertise, and experiences are brought to the table, power dynamics and inequities are not necessarily discussed or centered in cooperative participatory research. Transformative participatory action research (PAR) builds on cooperative participatory research by centering issues of power and oppression and committing to actions based on the needs of the marginalized or least powerful. In PAR, "the role of the researchers [is emphasized] as a change agent who establishes conditions for liberating dialogue with . . . oppressed groups and the political production of knowledge" (Mertens, 2010, p. 238). In other words, all of the coresearchers are working together to address and dismantle power structures that oppress, marginalize, and create inequities. Again, librarians might embark on participatory systematic inquiry with the best of intentions, but they may have

internalized some problematic practices that might prevent them from fully integrating diverse stakeholders into their inquiry work. Actionable Intelligence for Social Policy (2020) has created an incredibly useful toolkit that covers racially equitable data practices and provides examples of positive and problematic practices throughout the data life cycle. For example, in the planning phase, a positive practice is including diverse representatives. However, this can be problematic when they are treated as token representation or if their presence is simply performative (Actionable Intelligence for Social Policy, 2020, p. 16). As Mertens (2007) reminds us, "participation can be built into a project in ways that do or do not reflect cultural competency" (p. 220).

At this point, you might be wondering if we are anti–quantitative research and methods. The answer is, no, we are not. However, we think there are some limitations to relying solely on quantitative methods for race-centered, equity-minded systematic inquiry. As we discussed in chapter 5, early race-centered research in academic libraries relied heavily on quantitative methods, exploring the ways in which BIPOC students used libraries. In some cases, these studies found that BIPOC students were as likely or more likely to use libraries than their White peers (Whitmire, 1999, 2003). This finding is, of course, positive. However, it does not highlight potential differences in experiences between students with different racial/ethnic backgrounds. The students in our study were regular library users throughout their lives, including in college. However, many of them expressed having racialized experiences in libraries, including explicit acts of discrimination and microaggressions, that might not have surfaced if we had relied primarily on quantitative research. Furthermore, even if quantitative research uncovered that these students had racialized experiences, we likely would not have been able to capture the details of these experiences, including how they affected the students. Quantitative data can be an excellent starting point in undertaking race-centered, equity-minded research, as highlighted by McNair et al. (2020). If we are not regularly examining the data that we collect about how users are interacting with our libraries and disaggregating that data by race or ethnicity, we will not be aware of racialized issues that might require further exploration.

A CONCLUDING THOUGHT ON DISSEMINATION AND DISCOVERABILITY

As we mentioned earlier in this chapter, library colleagues across the country might be conducting equity-minded, race-centered evaluation and assessment that is not being widely disseminated because the intent of this work is for local improvement. Although libraries might share this work with their communities through their websites or other local platforms, this work will not be easily accessible to other colleagues who are using various search tools, such as Google, Google Scholar, or proprietary LIS databases, for exploration and discovery. Furthermore, if publication is not a requirement of one's position, undertaking the time and labor to write a manuscript, submit to a journal, undergo the peer-review process, and complete revisions will likely not be a priority. However, the lack of widespread dissemination of local assessment and evaluation work means that the profession does not have access to or the opportunity to benefit from this valuable work, which could be used to inform the practices at other libraries. A potential solution would be for ALA to host a repository of equity-minded, race-centered research, scholarship, evaluation, and assessment that could be searched by librarians, library staff, library faculty, library students, and others who are interested in creating more inclusive, equitable, just, and antiracist professional library environments. Such a repository could be actively promoted by the various ALA divisions (e.g., American Association of School Librarians, Association of College and Research Libraries, Public Library Association), as many LIS colleagues who hold membership in ALA find their homes at the division level.

RECOMMENDED READING

Actionable Intelligence for Social Policy. (2020). *A toolkit for centering racial equity within data integration.* The Annie E. Casey Foundation. https://www.aecf.org/resources/a-toolkit-for -centering-racial-equity-within-data-integration/

Nelson, J., & Brooks, L. (2016). *Racial equity toolkit: An opportunity to operationalize equity.* Government Alliance on Race and Equity. https://racialequity alliance.org/wp-content/uploads/2015/10/GARE -Racial_Equity_Toolkit.pdf

Sonnie, A. (2018, April). *Advancing racial equity in public libraries: Case studies from the field.* Government Alliance on Race and Equity. https://www.racialequityalliance.org/wp -content/uploads/2018/04/GARE_Libraries Report_Issue-Paper-April-2018.pdf

NOTES

1. Saad (2020) defines White saviorism as "the belief that people with white privilege, who see themselves as superior in capability and intelligence, have an obligation to 'save' BIPOC from their supposed inferiority and helplessness" (p. 149).

2. As mentioned in previous chapters, Bonilla-Silva (2018) uses the phrase color-blind, but we have chosen to use the less ableist term color-evasive based on the work of Annamma et al. (2017).

REFERENCES

Accardi, M. T. (2013). *Feminist pedagogy for library instruction*. Library Juice Press.

Accardi, M. T., Drabinski, E., & Kumbier, A. (Eds.). (2010). *Critical library instruction: Theories and methods*. Library Juice Press.

ACRL Association of College and Research Libraries. (2015). *Framework for information literacy for higher education*. ALA. http://www .ala.org/acrl/standards/ilframework

Actionable Intelligence for Social Policy. (2020). *A toolkit for centering racial equity within data integration*. The Annie E. Casey Foundation. https://www.aecf.org/resources/a-toolkit-for -centering-racial-equity-within-data-integration/

Agosto, D. E., & Hughes-Hassell, S. (2005). People, places, and questions: An investigation of the everyday life information-seeking behaviors of urban young adults. *Library and Information Science Research*, 27, 141–163.

Akua, C. (2012). *Education for transformation: The keys to releasing the genius of African American students*. Imani Enterprises.

Akua, C. (2015). *Honoring our ancestral obligations: 7 Steps to Black student success*. Imani Enterprises.

ALA American Library Association. (1939). *Library bill of rights*. Last updated January 29, 2019. https://www.ala.org/advocacy/intfreedom/ librarybill

ALA honors African Americans who fought library segregation. (2018, July 3). *American Libraries*. https://americanlibrariesmagazine.org/blogs/ the-scoop/ala-honors-african-americans-who -fought-library-segregation/

Alabi, J. (2015a). Racial microaggressions in academic libraries: Results of a survey of minority and non-minority librarians. *Journal of Academic Librarianship*, 41(1), 57–53.

Alabi, J. (2015b). "This actually happened": An analysis of librarians' responses to a survey about racial microaggressions. *Journal of Library Administration*, 55(3), 179–191.

Alabi, J. (2018). From hostile to inclusive: Strategies for improving the racial climate of academic libraries. *Library Trends*, 67(1), 131–146.

ALISE Association of Library and Information Science Education. (2020). *2020 Statistical report: Trends and key indicators in library and information science*. https://www.alise.org/statistical-report

Anderson, M. D. (2019, February 26). *Beyond slavery and the civil rights movement: Teachers should be integrating black history into their lessons*. NBC News. https://www.nbcnews.com/news/nbcblk/ beyond-slavery-civil-rights-movement-teachers -should-be-integrating-black-n976161

Annamma, S. A, Jackson, D. D., & Morrison, D. (2017). Conceptualizing color-evasiveness: Using dis/ability critical race theory to expand a color-blind racial ideology in education and society. *Race Ethnicity and Education*, 20(2), 147–162.

Arcidiacono, P., Kinsler, J., & Ransom, T. (2016). *Legacy and athlete preferences at Harvard* (Working Paper 26316). National Bureau of Economic Research. http://www.nber.org/ papers/w26316

Barton, P. E., & Coley, R. J. (2009). *Parsing the achievement gap II* (Policy Information Report).

Educational Testing Service. https://files.eric.ed.gov/fulltext/ED505163.pdf

Bauer, K. (Ed.). (1998). *Campus climate: Understanding the critical components of today's colleges and universities* (New directions for institutional research, no. 98). Jossey-Bass.

Bauman, D. (2018, November 14). Hate crimes on campuses are rising, new FBI data show. *The Chronicle of Higher Education.* https://www.chronicle.com/article/hate-crimes-on-campuses-are-rising-new-fbi-data-show/

Beasley, M. A. (2011). *Opting out: Losing the potential of America's young Black elite.* University of Chicago Press.

Beasley, M. M. (2017). Performing refuge/restoration: The role of libraries in the African American Community—Ferguson, Baltimore and Dorchester. *Performance Research, 22*(1), 75–81.

Beilin, I. (2017). *The academic research library's White past and present.* In G. Schlesselman-Tarango (Ed.), Topographies of Whiteness: Mapping Whiteness in library and information science (pp. 79–98). Library Juice Press.

Bell, D. A. (1980). *Brown v. Board of Education* and the interest-convergence dilemma. *Harvard Law Review, 93*(3), 518–533.

Bensimon, E. M. (2005). Closing the achievement gap in higher education: An organizational learning perspective. *New Directions for Higher Education, 131,* 99–111.

Bishop, R. S. (1982). *Shadow and substance: Afro-American experience in contemporary children's fiction.* National Council on Teachers of English.

Bonilla-Silva, E. (2018). *Racism without racists: Color-blind racism and the persistence of racial inequality in America* (5th ed.). Rowman & Littlefield.

Bourg, C. (2014, March 3). The unbearable whiteness of librarianship. *Feral Librarian.* https://chrisbourg.wordpress.com/2014/03/03/the-unbearable-whiteness-of-librarianship/

Bowers, J., Crowe, K., & Keeran, P. (2017). "If you want the history of a White man, you go to the library": Critiquing our legacy, addressing our collections gaps. *Collection Management, 42*(3–4), 159–179.

Brook, F., Ellenwood, D., & Lazzaro, A. E. (2015). In pursuit of antiracist social justice: Denaturalizing whiteness in the academic library. *Library Trends, 64*(2), 246–284.

Brown, T. M. (2007). Culture, gender and subjectivities: Computer and internet restrictions in a high school library. *Journal of Access Services, 4*(3/4), 1–26.

Buchmann, C., Condron, D. J., & Roscigno, V. J. (2010). Shadow education, American style: Test preparation, the SAT and college enrollment. *Social Forces, 89*(2), 435–461.

Bunner, T. (2017). When we listen: Using student voices to design culturally responsive and just schools. *Knowledge Quest, 45*(3), 38–45.

Burke, M. (2019). *Colorblind racism.* Polity.

Burnette, D. (2020, June 18). Schools or police: In some cities, a reckoning on spending priorities. *Education Week.* https://www.edweek.org/leadership/schools-or-police-in-some-cities-a-reckoning-on-spending-priorities/2020/06

Cabrera, A. F., Nora, A., Terenzini, P. T., Pascarella, E., & Hagedorn, L. S. (1999). Campus racial climate and the adjustment of students to college: A comparison between White students and African-American students. *Journal of Higher Education, 70*(2), 134–160.

Camera, L. (2019, February 26). White students get more K–12 funding than students of color: Report. *U.S. News and World Report.* https://www.usnews.com/news/education-news/articles/2019-02-26/white-students-get-more-k-12-funding-than-students-of-color-report

Camera, L. (2020, June 12). The end of police in schools. *U.S. News and World Report.* https://www.usnews.com/news/the-report/articles/

2020-06-12/schools-districts-end-contracts -with-police-amid-ongoing-protests

Cartwright, M. (2019). Timbuktu. In *World History Encyclopedia*. WorldHistory.org. https:// www.ancient.eu/Timbuktu/

Celano, D., & Neuman, S. B. (2001). *The role of public libraries in children's literacy development: An evaluation report*. Pennsylvania Library Association.

Chancellor, R. L. (2017). Libraries as pivotal community spaces in times of crisis. *Urban Library Journal*, 23(1), n.p.

Chang, M. J., Chang, J. C., & Ledesma, M. C. (2005). Beyond magical thinking: Doing the real work of diversifying our institutions. *About Campus*, 10(2), 9–16.

Chapman, J., Daly, E., Forte, A., King, I., Yang, B. W., & Zabala, P. (2020). *Understanding the experiences and needs of Black students at Duke* [Report]. DukeSpace, Duke University Libraries. https:// dukespace.lib.duke.edu/dspace/handle/10161/ 20753

Clarke, J. H. (2012). Partnering with IT to help disadvantaged students achieve academic success. *Public Services Quarterly*, 8(3), 208–226.

Clayton, E. (n.d.). Where did writing begin? In *A history of writing*. British Library. https:// www.bl.uk/history-of-writing/articles/where -did-writing-begin

Clotfelter, C. (2004). *After Brown: The rise and retreat of school desegregation*. Princeton University Press.

Coker, E. (2015). *Certified teacher-librarians, library quality and student achievement in Washington state public schools: The Washington state school library impact study*. Washington Library Media Association. https://wala.memberclicks.net/assets/ WLMA/Advocacy/wslitreport_final%20 revised7_14_15.pdf

Cooke, N. A., & Hill, R. F. (2017). Considering cultural competence. *Knowledge Quest*, 45(3), 54–61.

Cox, A., Gruber, A. M., & Neuhaus, C. (2019). Complexities of demonstrating library value: An exploratory study of research consultations. *portal: Libraries and the Academy*, 19(4), 577–590.

Cunningham, S., Guss, S., & Stout, J. (2019). Challenging the "good fit" narrative: Creating inclusive recruitment practices in academic libraries. In *Recasting the narrative: Proceedings of the Association of College and Research Libraries Conference, Cleveland, OH, April 10–13, 2019* (pp. 12–21). Association of College & Research Libraries.

Curry, D. A. (1994). Your worries ain't like mine: African American librarians and the pervasiveness of racism, prejudice and discrimination in academe. *The Reference Librarian*, 21(45–46), 299–311.

Darling-Hammond, L., & Dintersmith, T. (2017, August 2). A basic flaw in the argument against affirmative action. In V. Strauss, Actually, we still need affirmative action for African Americans in college admissions. Here's why. *The Washington Post*. https://www.washingtonpost.com/news/ answer-sheet/wp/2017/08/02/actually-we-still -need-affirmative-action-for-african-americans-in -college-admissions-heres-why/

Department for Professional Employees, AFL-CIO. (2020). *Library professionals: Facts and figures— 2020 Fact sheet*. https://www.dpeaflcio.org/fact sheets/library-professionals-facts-and-figures #_ednref15

Diliberti, M., Jackson, M., Correa, S., Padgett, Z., & Hansen, R. (2019). *Crime, violence, discipline, and safety in U.S. public schools: Findings from the School Survey on Crime and Safety: 2017–18: First look* (NCES 2019-061). National Center for Education Statistics. https://nces.ed.gov/pubs2019/2019061 .pdf

Dreilinger, D. (2020, October 14). *America's gifted education programs have a race problem. Can it be fixed?* NBC News. https://www.nbcnews.com/ news/education/america-s-gifted-education -programs-have-race-problem-can-it-n1243143

Dunbar, A. W. (2008). *Critical race information theory: Applying a CRITical race lens to information studies* (Publication No. 3357343) [Doctoral dissertation, University of California, Los Angeles]. ProQuest Dissertations.

Duster, T. (2009, Fall). The long path to higher education for African Americans. *Thought and Action*, 99–110.

EdBuild. (2019, February). *$23 Billion* [Report]. https://edbuild.org/content/23-billion/full-report.pdf

El-Abbadi, M. (n.d.). Library of Alexandria. In *Britannica*. https://www.britannica.com/topic/Library-of-Alexandria

Elmborg, J. (2006). Critical information literacy: Implications for instructional practice. *Journal of Academic Librarianship*, 32(2), 192–199.

Elteto, S., Jackson, R. M., & Lim, A. (2008). Is the library a "welcoming space"? An urban academic library and diverse student experiences. *portal: Libraries and the Academy*, 8(3), 325–337.

Espinal, I. (2001). A new vocabulary for inclusive librarianship: Applying whiteness theory to our profession. In L. Castillo-Speed (Ed.), *The power of language = el poder de la palabra: Selected papers from the second REFORMA National Conference* (pp. 131–149). Libraries Unlimited.

Espinal, I., Sutherland, T., & Roh, C. (2018). A holistic approach for inclusive librarianship: Decentering whiteness in our profession. *Library Trends*, 67(1), 147–162.

Estes, Rick. (1960, December 15). Segregated libraries. *Library Journal*, 85, 4418–4421.

Evans, S. A. (2019). "Book nerds" united: The reading lives of diverse adolescents at the public library. *The International Journal of Information, Diversity, and Inclusion*, 3(2), 40–62.

Feagin, J. R. (2020). *The White racial frame: Centuries of framing and counter-framing* (3rd ed.). Routledge.

Fenwick, L. T. (2001). *Patterns of excellence: Policy perspectives on diversifying teaching and school leadership*. Southern Education Foundation. https://eric.ed.gov/?id=ED472206

Finkelstein, M. J., Conley, V. M., & Schuster, J. H. (2016, April). *Taking the measure of faculty diversity*. TIAA Institute. https://www.tiaainstitute.org/publication/taking-measure-faculty-diversity

Fish, R. E. (2017). The racialized construction of exceptionality: Experimental evidence of race/ethnicity effects on teachers' interventions. *Social Science Research*, 62, 317–334.

Fish, R. E. (2019). Standing out and sorting in: Exploring the role of racial composition in racial disparities in special education. *American Educational Research Journal*, 56(6), 2573–2608.

Folk, A. L. (2018). Drawing on students' funds of knowledge: Using identity and lived experience to join the conversation in research assignments. *Journal of Information Literacy*, 12(2), 44–59.

Folk, A. L. (2019). Reframing information literacy as academic cultural capital: A critical and equity-based foundation for practice, assessment, and scholarship. *College and Research Libraries*, 80(5), 658–673.

Ford, D. Y. (2006). Closing the achievement gap: How gifted education can help. *Gifted Child Today*, 29(4), 14–18.

Ford, D. Y. (2013). Gifted underrepresentation and prejudice: Learning from Allport and Merton. *Gifted Child Today*, 36(1), 62-67.

Ford, J. E., & Triplett, N. (2019, August 14). *E(race)ing inequities: Chronic absenteeism*. EdNC. https://www.ednc.org/eraceing-inequities-chronic-absenteeism/

Franke, R., & DeAngelo, L. (2018, April). *Degree attainment for Black students at HBCUs and PWIs: A propensity score matching approach* [Paper presentation]. Annual Conference of the American Educational Research Association, New York, NY.

Friedman, Z. (2019, March 12). Hollywood celebrities charged in major college admissions scandal. *Forbes*. https://www.forbes.com/sites/zackfriedman/2019/03/12/hollywood-celebrities-charged-in-major-college-admissions-scandal/?sh=1d2b18e11dc5

Frueh, S. (2020, July 9). *COVID-19 and Black communities*. The National Academies of Sciences, Engineering, and Medicine. https://www.nationalacademies.org/news/2020/07/covid-19-and-black-communities

Fultz, M. (2006). Black public libraries in the South in the era of de jure segregation. *Libraries and the Cultural Record*, 41(3), 337–359.

Galvan, A. (2015, June 3). Soliciting performance, hiding bias: Whiteness and librarianship. *In the Library with the Lead Pipe*. http://www.inthelibrarywiththeleadpipe.org/2015/soliciting-performance-hiding-bias-whiteness-and-librarianship/

Garrison, G. (2013, May 13). *Civil rights pioneer N. Q. Reynolds of Anniston, who was beaten by Klan in 1963, dies at 82*. Advance Local. https://www.al.com/living/2013/05/civil_rights_pioneer_nq_reynol.html

George Mwangi, C. A., Thelamour, B., Ezeofor, I., & Carpenter, A. (2018). "Black elephant in the room": Black students contextualizing campus racial climate within US racial climate. *Journal of College Student Development*, 59(4), 456–474.

Gershenson, S., Holt, S. B., & Papageorge, N. W. (2016). Who believes in me? The effect of student-teacher demographic match on teacher expectations. *Economics of Education Review*, 52, 209–224.

Gibson, A. N., Chancellor, R. L., Cooke, N. A., Dahlen, S. P., Lee, S. A., & Shorish, Y. L. (2017). Libraries on the frontlines: Neutrality and social justice. *Equality, Diversity and Inclusion*, 36(8), 751–766.

Gibson, A., Hughes-Hassell, S., & Threats, M. (2018). Critical race theory in the LIS curriculum. In J. Percell, L. C. Sarin, P. T. Jaeger, & J. C. Bertot (Eds.), *Re-envisioning the MLS: Perspectives on the future of library and information science education* (Vol. 44B, pp. 49–70). Emerald Publishing.

Giulietti, C., Vlassopoulos, M., & Tonin, M. (2019). Racial discrimination in local public services: A field experiment in the United States. *Journal of the European Economic Association*, 17(1), 165–204.

Gong, H., Japzon, A. C., & Chen, C. (2008). Public libraries and social capital in three New York City neighborhoods. *Tijdschrift voor Economische en Sociale Geografie*, 99(1), 65–83.

Goodman, A. H. (2008). Exposing race as an obsolete biological concept. In M. Pollock, *Everyday antiracism: Getting real about race in school* (pp. 4–7). New Press.

Gordon, E. K., Hawley, Z. B., Kobler, R. C., & Rork, J. C. (2020). The paradox of HBCU graduation rates [Preprint]. *Research in Higher Education*.

Gorman, A. *The hill we climb: An inaugural poem for the country*. Viking Books.

Grant, G. (2011). *Hope and despair in the American city: Why there are no bad schools in Raleigh*. Harvard University Press.

Griffiths, C., & Buttery, T. (2018, March 19). *The world's oldest centre of learning*. BBC. http://www.bbc.com/travel/gallery/20180318-the-worlds-oldest-centre-of-learning

Gusa, D. L. (2010). White institutional presence: The impact of whiteness on campus culture. *Harvard Educational Review*, 80(4), 464–489.

Hall, T. D. (2012). The Black body at the reference desk: Critical race theory and Black librarianship. In A. P. Jackson, J. C. Jefferson, & A. S. Nosakhere (Eds.), *The 21st-century Black librarian in America: Issues and challenges* (pp. 197–202). Scarecrow Press.

Harper, S. R., & Quaye, S. J. (2015). Making engagement equitable for students in U.S. higher education. In S. J. Quaye & S. R. Harper (Eds.), *Student engagement in higher education: Theoretical perspectives and practical approaches for diverse populations* (pp. 1–14). Routledge.

Harrell, M., & Menon, V. (2002, April). *Serving diverse library users: The multicultural studies librarian at an urban research university* [Paper presentation]. Diversity in Academic Libraries, University of Iowa, Iowa City, Iowa. http://www.lib.uiowa.edu/wwwarchive/cicdiversity/harrell.doc

Harvey, W. B., Harvey, A. M., & King, M. (2004). The impact of the *Brown v. Board of Education* decision on postsecondary participation of African Americans. *Journal of Negro Education*, 73(3), 328–340.

Hathcock, A. (2015, October 7). White librarianship in Blackface: Diversity initiatives in LIS. *In the Library with the Lead Pipe.* https://www.inthelibrarywiththeleadpipe.org/2015/lis-diversity/

Hathcock, A. M., & Sendaula, S. (2017). Mapping whiteness at the reference desk. In G. Schlesselman-Tarango (Ed.), *Topographies of Whiteness: Mapping Whiteness in library and information science* (pp. 247–256). Library Juice Press.

Haynes, B. (2006). *Black undergraduates in higher education: A historical perspective.* Metropolitan Universities, 17(2), 8–21.

Heitzeg, N. A. (2009). Education or incarceration: Zero tolerance policies and the school to prison pipeline. *Forum on Public Policy Online*, no. 2. https://eric.ed.gov/?id=EJ870076

Hines, S. (2019). Leadership development for academic librarians: Maintaining the status quo. *Canadian Journal of Academic Librarianship*, 4, 1–19.

Holmes, B., & Lichtenstein, A. (1998). Minority student success: Librarians as partners. *College and Research Libraries News*, 59(7), 496–498.

Honma, T. (2005). Trippin' over the color line: The invisibility of race in library and information studies. *InterActions: UCLA Journal of Education and Information Studies*, 1(2), n.p.

Horowitz, J. M., Brown, A., & Cox, K. (2019, April 9). *Race in America 2019.* Pew Research Center. https://www.pewresearch.org/social-trends/2019/04/09/race-in-america-2019/

Horrigan, J. (2015, September 15). *Libraries at the crossroads.* Pew Research Center. https://www.pewresearch.org/internet/2015/09/15/libraries-at-the-crossroads/

Howell, C., & Turner, S. E. (2004). Legacies in black and white: The racial composition of the legacy pool. *Research in Higher Education*, 45(4), 325–351.

Hudson, A. (2010). Measuring the impact of cultural diversity on desired mobile reference services. *Reference Services Review*, 38(2), 299–308.

Hudson, D. J. (2017). On "diversity" as anti-racism in library and information studies: A critique. *Journal of Critical Library and Information Studies*, 1(1), 1–36.

Hughes-Hassell, S. (2013). Designing effective library services for African American youth. *School Library Monthly*, 29(6), 11–13.

Hughes-Hassell, S., Barkley, H. A., and Koehler, E. (2009). Promoting equity in children's literacy instruction: Using a critical race theory framework to examine transitional books. *School Library Media Research*, 12, n.p.

Hughes-Hassell, S., Kumasi, K., Rawson, C. H., & Hitson, A. (2012). *Building a bridge to literacy for African American male youth: A call to action for the library community* [Report]. School of Information and Library Science, University of North Carolina at Chapel Hill.

Hughes-Hassell, S., & Lutz, C. (2006). What do you want to tell us about reading? A survey of the habits and attitudes of urban middle school students toward leisure reading. *Young Adult Library Services*, 4(2), 39–45.

Irizarry, Y. & Cohen, E. D. (2019). Of promise and penalties: How student racial-cultural markers shape teacher perceptions. *Race and Social Problems*, 11, 93–111.

Isensee, l. (2015, October 23). Why calling slaves "workers" is more than an editing error. NPR. https://www.npr.org/sections/ed/2015/10/23/

450826208/why-calling-slaves-workers-is-more -than-an-editing-error

JBHE *The Journal of Blacks in Higher Education*. (n.d.). *Key events in Black higher education: JBHE chronology of major landmarks in the progress of African Americans in higher education*. https://www .jbhe.com/chronology/

Johnson, C. A. (2010). Do public libraries contribute to social capital? A preliminary investigation into the relationship. *Library and Information Science Research*, 32, 147–155.

Johnson, U. (2013). *Psycho-academic holocaust: The special education and ADHD wars against Black boys*. Prince of Pan-Africanism Publishing.

Jones, V. L. (1945). *Problems of negro public high school libraries in selected southern cities*. [Doctoral dissertation, University of Chicago].

Katopol, P. F. (2012). Information anxiety and African-American students in a graduate education program. *Education Libraries*, 32(1/2), 5–14.

Kendi, I. X. (2019). *How to be an antiracist*. One World.

Kendrick, K. D., & Damasco, I. T. (2019). Low morale in ethnic and racial minority academic librarians: An experiential study. *Library Trends*, 68(2), 174–212.

King, S. (2016, January 29). Why Black History Month should never begin with slavery. *New York Daily News*. https://www.nydailynews .com/news/national/king-black-history-month -slavery-article-1.2513580

Knott, C. (2015). *Not free, not for all: Public libraries in the age of Jim Crow*. University of Massachusetts Press.

Kozol, J. (2005). *The shame of the nation: The restoration of apartheid schooling in America*. Crown Publishers.

Kuh, G. D., & Hall, J. E. (1993). Using cultural perspectives in student affairs. In G. D. Kuh (Ed.), *Cultural perspectives in student affairs work* (pp. 1–20). American College Personnel Association.

Kumasi, K. (2008). *Seeing white in black: Examining racial identity among African American youth in culturally responsive book club* (Publication No. 3344582) [Doctoral dissertation, Indiana University]. ProQuest Dissertations.

Kumasi, K. (2012). Roses in the concrete: A critical race perspective on urban youth and school libraries. *Knowledge Quest*, 40(4), 32–37.

Kumasi, K. (2013). "The library is like her house": Reimagining youth of color in LIS discourses. In A. Bernier (Ed.), *Transforming young adult services: A reader for our age* (pp. 103–113). ALA Neal-Schuman. Retrieved from Digital Commons@ Wayne State. http://digitalcommons.wayne .edu/slisfrp/95

Kumasi, K., & Hughes-Hassell, S. (2017). Shifting lenses on youth literacy and identity. *Knowledge Quest*, 45(3), 12–21.

Ladson-Billings, G. (1995). Toward a theory of culturally relevant pedagogy. *American Educational Research Journal*, 32(3), 465–491.

Ladson-Billings, G., & Tate, W. F. (1995). Toward a critical race theory of education. *Teachers College Record*, 97(1), 47–68.

Lambe, S. (2021, March 18). Operation varsity blues: A guide to the college admissions scandal. *ET*. https://www.etonline.com/operation-varsity -blues-a-guide-to-the-college-admissions -scandal-134135

Lance, K. C., & Kachel, D. E. (2018). Why school librarians matter: What years of research tell us. *Phi Delta Kappan*, 99(7), 15–20.

Leung, S. Y., & López-McKnight, J. R. (2020). Dreaming revolutionary futures: Critical race's centrality to ending White supremacy. *Communications in Information Literacy*, 14(1), 12–26.

Love, E. (2009). A simple step: Integrating library reference and instruction into previously established academic programs for minority students. *The Reference Librarian*, 50, 4–13.

Mabbott, C. (2017). The We Need Diverse Books campaign and critical race theory: Charlemae Rollins and the call for diverse children's books. *Library Trends*, 65(4), 508–522.

MacAdam, B., & Nichols, D. P. (1989). Peer information counseling: An academic library program for minority students. *Journal of Academic Librarianship*, 15, 204–209.

MacDonald, K. C. (n.d.). Wonders: Sankore Mosque [Episode]. In *The Road to Timbuktu*. PBS. https://www.pbs.org/wonders/Episodes/Epi5/5_wondr6.htm

Mallinckrodt, B., & Sedlacek, W. E. (1987). Undergraduate retention and the use of campus facilities by race. *NASPA Journal*, 24(3), 28–32.

Maloney, M.M. (2012). Cultivating community, promoting inclusivity: Collections as a fulcrum for targeted outreach. *New Library World*, 113(5/6), 281–289.

Manchester, J. (2021, May 17). Republicans seize on conservative backlash against critical race theory. *The Hill*. https://thehill.com/homenews/campaign/553631-republicans-seize-on-conservative-backlash-against-critical-race-theory

Matthews, A. (2020). Racialized youth in the public library: Systemic racism through a critical theory lens. *Theory and Research*, 15(1), 1–17.

Mbekeani-Wiley, M. (2017, February). *Handcuffs in hallways: The state of policing in Chicago public schools* [Report]. Sargent Shriver National Center on Poverty Law. https://www.povertylaw.org/wp-content/uploads/2020/07/handcuffs-in-hallways-amended-rev1.pdf

McGhee, H. (2021). *The sum of us: What racism costs everyone and how we can prosper together*. One World.

McNair, T. B., Bensimon, E. M., & Malcom-Piqueux, L. (2020). *From equity talk to equity walk: Expanding practitioner knowledge for racial justice in higher education*. Jossey-Bass.

Mehra, B. (2021). Enough crocodile tears! Libraries moving beyond performative antiracist politics. *Library Quarterly*, 91(2), 137–149.

Mercer, M. (2020, August 20). *Black history instruction gets new emphasis in many states*. The Pew Charitable Trusts. https://www.pewtrusts.org/en/research-and-analysis/blogs/stateline/2020/08/20/black-history-instruction-gets-new-emphasis-in-many-states

Mertens, D. M. (2007). Transformative paradigm: Mixed methods and social justice. *Journal of Mixed Methods Research*, 1(3), 212–225.

Mertens, D. M. (2010). *Research and evaluation in education and psychology* (3rd ed.). Sage Publications.

Miller, R. (2012). *Teacher absence as a leading indicator of student achievement: New national data offer opportunity to examine cost of teacher absence relative to learning loss*. Center for American Progress. https://www.americanprogress.org/wp-content/uploads/2012/11/TeacherAbsence-6.pdf

Mortimore, J. M., & Wall, A. (2009). Motivating African-American students through information literacy instruction: Exploring the link between encouragement and academic self-concept. *Reference Librarian*, 50(1), 29–42.

Moses, Y. T. (1999). Race, higher education, and American society. *Journal of Anthropological Research*, 55(2), 265–277.

Museus, S. D., Ravello, J. N., & Vega, B.E. (2012). The campus racial culture: A critical race counter-story. In S. D. Museus & U. M. Jayakumar (Eds.), *Creating campus cultures: Fostering success among racially diverse student populations* (pp. 28–45). Routledge.

Nash, M. A. (2019, November 8). The dark history of land-grant universities. *The Washington Post*. https://www.washingtonpost.com/outlook/2019/11/08/dark-history-land-grant-universities/

NCES National Center for Education Statistics. (2019a). Indicator 7: Racial/ethnic concentration in public schools. In *Status and trends in the*

REFERENCES

education of racial and ethnic groups. https://nces .ed.gov/programs/raceindicators/indicator_rbe .asp

NCES National Center for Education Statistics. (2019b). Indicator 19: College participation rates. In *Status and trends in the education of racial and ethnic groups.* https://nces.ed.gov/programs/ raceindicators/indicator_REA.asp

NCES National Center for Education Statistics. (2019c). Indicator 23: Postsecondary graduation rates. In *Status and trends in the education of racial and ethnic groups.* https://nces.ed.gov/programs/ raceindicators/indicator_red.asp

NCES National Center for Education Statistics. (2019d). Table 306.10. Total fall enrollment in degree-granting postsecondary institutions, by level of enrollment, sex, attendance status, and race/ethnicity or nonresident alien status of student: Selected years, 1976 through 2018. In *Digest of education statistics.* https://nces.ed.gov/ programs/digest/d19/tables/dt19_306.10.asp

NCES National Center for Education Statistics. (2019e). Table 313.20. Fall enrollment in degree-granting historically Black colleges and universities, by sex of student and level and control of institution: Selected years, 1976 through 2018. In *Digest of education statistics.* https://nces.ed.gov/programs/digest/d19/tables/ dt19_313.20.asp

NCES National Center for Education Statistics. (2019f). *Web tables — Advanced placement, international baccalaureate, and dual-enrollment courses: Availability, participation, and related outcomes for 2009 ninth-graders: 2013.* https://nces .ed.gov/pubs2019/2019430.pdf

NCES National Center for Education Statistics. (2020). *Fast facts: Race ethnicity of college faculty.* https:// nces.ed.gov/fastfacts/display.asp?id=61

NCES National Center for Education Statistics. (2021a). Indicator 22: Hate crime incidents at postsecondary institutions. In *The Condition of*

Education 2021. https://nces.ed.gov/programs/ crimeindicators/ind_22.asp

NCES National Center for Education Statistics. (2021b). Racial/ethnic enrollment in public schools. In *The Condition of Education 2021.* https:// nces.ed.gov/programs/coe/indicator_cge.asp

Nelson, J., & Brooks, L. (2016). *Racial equity toolkit: An opportunity to operationalize equity.* Government Alliance on Race and Equity. https://racialequity alliance.org/wp-content/uploads/2015/10/GARE -Racial_Equity_Toolkit.pdf

Neuman, S. B., & Moland, N. (2019). Book deserts: The consequences of income segregation on children's access to print. *Urban Education,* 54(1), 126–147.

Noguera, P. A. (2008). *The trouble with black boys . . . and other reflections on race, equity, and the future of public education.* Jossey Bass.

Norlin, E. (2001). University goes back to basics to reach minority students. *American Libraries,* 32(7), 60–62.

Norlin, E., & Morris, P. (1999). Developing proactive partnerships: Minority cultural centers. *The Reference Librarian,* 67/68, 147–160.

O'Dell, L. (n.d.). Smitherman, Andrew J (1885–1961). *The encyclopedia of Oklahoma history and culture.* Oklahoma Historical Society. https://www .okhistory.org/publications/enc/entry.php? entry=SM008

Oklahoma Historical Society. (n.d.). *Tulsa Star* [Collection home page]. The Gateway to Oklahoma Society [Website]. https://gateway .okhistory.org/explore/collections/TULSA/

Okun, T. (2021). *White supremacy culture characteristics.* White Supremacy Culture. https://www.white supremacyculture.info/characteristics.html

Oluo, I. (2019). *So you want to talk about race.* Seal Press.

Orfield, G. & Lee, C. (2004). *Brown at 50: King's dream or Plessy's nightmare?* The Civil Rights Project, Harvard University. https://civilrightsproject

.ucla.edu/research/k-12-education/integration -and-diversity/brown-at-50-king2019s-dream-or -plessy2019s-nightmare/orfield-brown-50-2004. pdf

Overbey, T. A. (2020). Food deserts, libraries and urban communities: What is the connection? *Public Library Quarterly*, 39(1), 37–49.

Owusu-Ansah, F. E., & Mji, G. (2013). African indigenous knowledge and research. *African Journal of Disability*, 2(1), 1–5.

Pagowsky, N., & McElroy, K. (Eds.). (2016a). *Critical library pedagogy handbook: Vol. 1. Essays and workbook activities*. Association of College & Research Libraries.

Pagowsky, N., & McElroy, K. (Eds.). (2016b). *Critical library pedagogy handbook: Vol. 2. Lesson plans*. Association of College & Research Libraries.

Palomba, C. A., & Banta, T. W. (1999). *Assessment essentials: Planning, implementing, and improving assessment in higher education*. Jossey-Bass.

Pashia, A. (2016). Black Lives Matter in information literacy. *Radical Teacher*, 106, 141–143.

Pawley, C. (2006). Unequal legacies: Race and multiculturalism in the LIS curriculum. *Library Quarterly*, 76(2), 149–168.

Pierce, C. (1970). Offensive mechanisms. In F. Barbour (Ed.), *The Black seventies* (pp. 265–282). Porter Sargent.

Pirtle, W. (2019, April 23). The other segregation: The public focuses its attention on divides between schools, while tracking has created separate and unequal education systems within single schools. *The Atlantic*. https://www.theatlantic .com/education/archive/2019/04/gifted-and -talented-programs-separate-students-race/ 587614/

Preston, C. (1998). Perceptions of discriminatory practices and attitudes: A survey of African American librarians. *College and Research Libraries*, 59(5), 433–444.

Pribesh, S., Gavigan, K., & Dickinson, G. (2011). The access gap: Poverty and characteristics of school library media centers. *Library Quarterly*, 81(2), 143–160.

Prison Policy Initiative. (2020). *Mass incarceration: The whole pie 2020*. https://www.prisonpolicy.org/ reports/pie2020.html

Ramirez, M. H. (2015). Being assumed not to be: A critique of Whiteness as an archival imperative. *American Archivist*, 78(2), 339–356.

Rankin, S. R., & Reason, R. D. (2005). Differing perceptions: How students of color and white students perceive campus climate for under-represented groups. *Journal of College Student Development*, 46(1), 43–61.

Rapchak, M. (2019). That which cannot be named: The absence of race in the Framework for Information Literacy for Higher Education. *Journal of Radical Librarianship*, 5, 173–196.

Ray, P. (2015). *Defining defiance: African-American middle school students' perspectives on the impact of teachers' disciplinary referrals* (Publication No. 3723083) [Doctoral dissertation, Loyola Marymount University]. ProQuest Dissertations.

Riddle, T., & Sinclair, S. (2019). Racial disparities in school-based disciplinary actions are associated with county-level rates of racial bias. *PNAS*, 116(17), 8255–8260.

Rideout, V., & Katz., V. (2016, February 3). *Opportunity for all? Technology and learning in lower-income families* (A report of the Families and Media Project). Joan Ganz Cooney Center. https:// joanganzcooneycenter.org/publication/ opportunity-for-all-technology-and-learning -in-lower-income-families/

Robinson, B. (2019). No holds barred: Policing and security in the public library. *In the Library with the Lead Pipe*. https://www.inthelibrarywiththe leadpipe.org/2019/no-holds-barred/

Robinson, C. C. (1970). First by circumstance. In E. J. Josey (Ed.), *The Black librarian in America* (pp. 275–283). Scarecrow.

Rosa, K., & Henke, K. (2017). *2017 ALA demographic study*. American Library Association, Office for Research and Statistics. http://www.ala.org/tools/sites/ala.org.tools/files/content/Draft%20of%20Member%20Demographics%20Survey%2001-11-2017.pdf

Russ-Eft, D., & Preskill, H. (2009). *Evaluation in organizations: A systematic approach to enhancing learning, performance, and change*. Basic Books.

Saad, L. F. (2020). *Me and white supremacy: Combat racism, change the world, and become a good ancestor*. Sourcebooks.

Sammons, V. O. (1990). *Blacks in science and medicine*. Hemisphere.

Schlesselman-Tarango, G. (2016). The legacy of Lady Bountiful: White women in the library. *Library Trends*, 64(4), 667–686.

Selby, M. (2019). *Freedom libraries: The untold story of libraries for African Americans in the South*. Rowman & Littlefield.

Sentencing Project. (2016). *Policy brief: Racial disparities in youth commitments and arrests*. https://www.sentencingproject.org/publications/racial-disparities-in-youth-commitments-and-arrests/

Shachaf, P., & Snyder, M. (2007). The relationship between cultural diversity and user needs in virtual reference services. *Journal of Academic Librarianship*, 33(3), 361–367.

Shin, Y. (2012). Do Black children benefit more from small classes? Multivariate instrumental variable estimators with ignorable missing data. *Journal of Educational and Behavioral Statistics*, 37(4), 543–574.

Shoge, R. C. (2003). The library as place in the lives of African Americans. In H. A. Thompson (Ed.), *Learning to make a difference: Proceedings of the Eleventh National Conference of the Association of College and Research Libraries, April 10–13, 2003, Charlotte, NC* (n.p.). Association of College and Research Libraries.

Silva, D. (2019, September 30). *Study on Harvard finds 43 percent of white students are legacy, athletes, related to donors or staff*. NBC News. https://www.nbcnews.com/news/us-news/study-harvard-finds-43-percent-white-students-are-legacy-athletes-n1060361

Simmons-Welburn, J. & Welburn, W. C. (2001). Cultivating partnerships/realizing diversity. *Journal of Library Administration*, 33(1/2), 5–19.

Sin, S. J. (2011). Neighborhood disparities in access to information resources: Measuring and mapping U.S. public libraries' funding and service landscapes. *Library and Information Science Research*, 33(1), 41–53.

Solórzano, D., Ceja, M., & Yosso, T. (2000). Critical race theory, racial microaggressions, and campus racial climate: The experiences of African American college students. *Journal of Negro Education*, 69(1/2), 60–73.

Sonnie, A. (2018, April) *Advancing racial equity in public libraries: Case studies from the field*. Government Alliance on Race and Equity. https://www.racialequityalliance.org/wp-content/uploads/2018/04/GARE_LibrariesReport_Issue-Paper-April-2018.pdf

Spink, A., & Cole, C. (2001). Information and poverty: Information-seeking channels used by African American low-income households. *Library and Information Science Research*, 23(1), 45–65.

Stauffer, S. M. (2020). Educating for Whiteness: Applying critical race theory's revisionist history in library and information science research: A methodology paper. *Journal of Education for Library and Information Science*, 61(4), 452–462.

Stewart, B., Ju, B., & Kendrick, K. D. (2019). Racial climate and inclusiveness in academic libraries: Perceptions of welcomeness among Black college students. *Library Quarterly*, 89(1), 16–33.

Stewart, M. (2020, August 18). Symbols matter: Colleges and universities respond to movement against racist imagery and namesakes. *Insight Into Diversity*. https://www.insightintodiversity.com/symbols-matter-colleges-and-universities

-respond-to-movement-against-racist-imagery
-and-namesakes/

Tatum, B. D. (2017). *Why are all the black kids sitting together in the cafeteria: And other conversations about race.* Basic Books.

Tulsa City-County Library. (2018). Section 2: The 1921 Tulsa race massacre. In *TCCL remembers: Commemorating Tulsa's 1921 race massacre with education, empathy, and healing* [Exhibit]. https://www.tulsalibrary.org/1921-tulsa-race-massacre

Walter, S. (2005). Moving beyond collections: Academic library outreach to multicultural student centers. *Reference Services Review*, 33(4), 438–458.

Warner, J. N. (2001). Moving beyond Whiteness in North American academic libraries. *Libri*, 51, 167–172.

Weissman, S. (2019, August 14). Pew study: Faculty-student diversity divide persists. *Diverse Issues in Higher Education*. https://diverseeducation.com/article/152333/

Whitmire, E. (1999). Racial differences in the academic library experiences of undergraduates. *Journal of Academic Librarianship*, 25(1), 33–37.

Whitmire, E. (2003). Cultural diversity and undergraduates' academic library use. *Journal of Academic Librarianship*, 29(3), 148–161.

Whitmire, E. (2004). The campus racial climate and undergraduates' perceptions of the academic library. *portal: Libraries and the Academy*, 4(3), 363–378.

Whitmire, E. (2006). African American undergraduates and the university academic library. *Journal of Negro Education*, 75(1), 60–66.

Wiegand, W. A. (2017). Any ideas? The American Library Association and the desegregation of public libraries in the American South. *Libraries: Culture, History, and Society*, 1(1), 1–22.

Wiegand, W. A. (2021). Race and school librarianship in the Jim Crow South, 1954–1970: The untold story of Carrie Coleman Robinson as a case study. *Library Quarterly*, 91(3), 254–268.

Wiegand, W. A., & Wiegand, S. A. (2018). *The desegregation of public libraries in the Jim Crow South: Civil rights and local activism.* Louisiana State University Press.

Wilder, C. S. (2013). *Ebony and ivy: Race, slavery, and the troubled history of America's universities.* Bloomsbury Publishing.

Williams, J., & Ashley, D. (2004). *I'll find a way or make one: A tribute to historically Black colleges and universities.* Amistad Press.

Wise, A. (2020, September 17). *Trump announces "patriotic education" commission, a largely political move.* NPR. https://www.npr.org/2020/09/17/914127266/trump-announces-patriotic-education-commission-a-largely-political-move

Yosso, T. J. (2005). Whose culture has capital? A critical race theory discussion of community cultural wealth. *Race Ethnicity and Education*, 8(1), 69–91.

Zimmerman, J. (2020, October 11). Ethnic studies can't make up for whitewashed history in classrooms. *The Washington Post*. https://www.washingtonpost.com/outlook/2020/10/11/ethnic-studies-cant-make-up-whitewashed-history-classrooms/

Zulu, I. M. (1993). The ancient Kemetic roots of library and information science. In *Culture keepers: Enlightening and empowering our communities: Proceedings of the First National Conference of African American Librarians, September 4–6, 1992, Columbus, OH* (pp. 246–266). The Black Caucus of the American Library Association. https://files.eric.ed.gov/fulltext/ED382204.pdf

ABOUT THE AUTHORS

TRACEY OVERBEY is assistant professor and social sciences librarian at The Ohio State University Libraries. She earned a master's degree in library and information science from the University of Pittsburgh. Her research interests include issues related to food desert communities and educating and exposing marginalized students to information literacy using library resources. She won an organizational award for implementing a seed library at The Ohio State University Libraries for students to obtain seeds from the library to plant fresh produce within their residence halls. This initiative helped those students and faculty who live in food desert communities. She has also won state and local grants that expose students who live within economically strained communities to science, technology, engineering, and math (STEM) resources through programming and hands-on explorations. In addition, she serves on the Executive Board for the Black Caucus of the American Library Association, has published in *Public Library Quarterly* and *International Journal of Environmental Health Research*, and has presented papers at conferences of the International Federation of Library Associations (IFLA) and the Association of College and Research Libraries (ACRL).

AMANDA L. FOLK is an associate professor and head of the Teaching and Learning department at The Ohio State University Libraries. She earned her PhD in social and comparative analysis in education from the University of Pittsburgh's School of Education. Her research interests include exploring the sociocultural nature of information literacy and implications for teaching and learning, as well as examining the academic and library experiences of student populations that have traditionally been marginalized in higher education in the United States. In addition to serving as the editor in chief for the *Journal of Academic Librarianship*, she has been published in *College and Research Libraries*, *portal: Libraries and the Academy, College and Undergraduate Libraries*, the *Journal of Library Administration*, and *International Information and Library Review*. She was the recipient of the 2020 ACRL Instruction Section's Ilene F. Rockman Instruction Publication of the Year Award.

INDEX

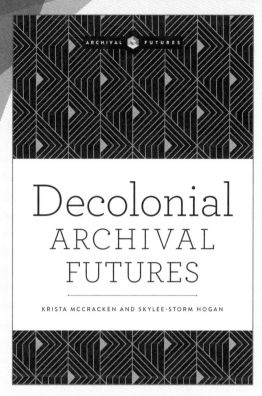
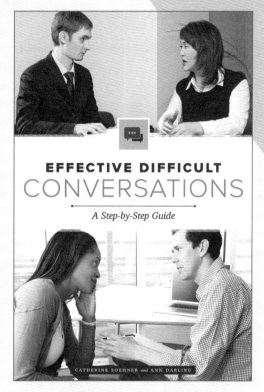

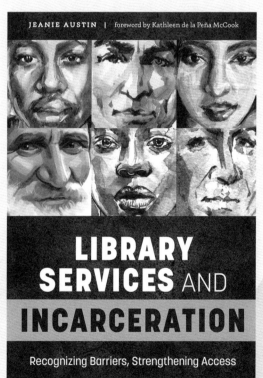